GOD WITH US

CHRIST IN TYPE, FORM & PROPHECY IN THE OLD TESTAMENT

Paul M. Ethington

God With Us © 2019 by Paul Ethington.

All rights reserved. No part of this book may be reproduced in any form or by any electronic or mechanical means including information storage and retrieval systems, without permission in writing from the author. The only exception is by a reviewer, who may quote short excerpts in a review.

Author: Paul M. Ethington

Unless otherwise indicated, all Scripture quotations are from the Holy bible, The New King James Version, Copyright © 1982 by Thomas Nelson, Inc.

Printed in the United States of America

First printing Dec 2019

SDBN 9781672125659

This book is dedicated to Dr. Ronald Hunter who was kind enough to read and critique my manuscript, and who has written a book on the subject of biblical typology entitled *Delightful Insights*, 2014.

TABLE OF CONTENTS

PREFACE 1

PART I - CHRIST IN TYPE: THAT WE MAY UNDERSTAND
    Introduction to Part I 4
1. The Covenant of Pieces 5
2. The Slavery in Egypt 7
3. The Tabernacle 9
4. The Passover and Day of Atonement 29
5. The Feast of Tabernacles 33
6. The Theme of "Firstborn" in the Bible 37
7. The Lives of Christ-like Men 41
        Job 43
        Noah 43
        Abraham 44
        Isaac 45
        Joseph 46
        Moses 47
        Boaz 49
        Samuel 52
        David 53
        Daniel 54
        Esther 56
        Jonah 57
        Hosea 58

PART II - CHRIST IN FORM: THAT WE MAY SEE
    Introduction to Part II 59
8. Christophany (The Angel of Jehovah) 63

PART III - CHRIST IN PROPHECY: THAT WE MAY BELIEVE
    Introduction to Part III 73
9. Messianic Prophecy in the Pentateuch
        Adam 77
        Noah 79
        Abraham 80
        Jacob and Judah 82

	Balaam	83
	Moses	84
	Job	86
10.	Messianic Prophecy Leading up to David	89
	Hannah and God's "Anointed One"	90
	Eli and the "Faithful Priest"	90
	Nathan and the Eternal Kingdom of David	91
11.	David & the Psalms	95
	The Rejection of Messiah (Psalm 118)	95
	The Betrayal of Messiah (Psalms 69 & 109)	98
	The Death & Resurrection of Messiah (Psalms 22 & 16)	101
	The Conquering King & Enthroned Messiah (Psalms 110 & 2)	103
	Messiah as Triumphant King (Psalms 68 & 72)	104
12.	Ninth & Eighth Century Prophets	107
	The Messiah as Teacher of Righteousness (Joel 2:23)	108
	The Messiah as the Second David (Hosea 3:4-5)	110
	The Messiah as the Raised House of David (Amos 9:11-15)	112
	The Messiah as the Breaker (Micah 2:12-13)	113
	The Messiah as the Coming Ruler (Micah 5:1-4)	115
13.	Isaiah	117
	A. Messiah as King	
	1. The Branch of the Lord (Isa 4:1)	117
	2. The Virgin Birth (Isa 7:1-16)	118
	3. The Wonderful Ruling Son)Isa 9:1-7)	119
	4. The Reign of Jessie's Son (Isa 11:1-16)	121
	B. Messiah as Servant	
	1. The Servant's Mission to the World (Isa 42:1-7; 49:1-6)	122
	2. The Servant's Humiliation (Isa 50:4-9)	125
	3. The Servant's Atonement (Isa 52:13-53:12)	126
	C. Messiah as the Consummation of All Things	
	1. Messiah as Healer (Isa 35:1-11)	127
	2. Messiah as Comforter (Isa 40:9-11)	127
	3. Messiah as a Gift to All Nations (Isa 55:3-5)	128
	4. Messiah as Proclaimer (Isa 6:1-3)	129
	5. Messiah as Conqueror (Isa 63:1-6)	130
14.	Seventh & Sixth Century Prophets	
	A. Jeremiah	131
	1. Messiah as the Lord of Our Righteousness (Jer 23:5-6)	132
	2. Messiah as the Priestly King (Jer 30:9,21)	132
	3. The Inviolable Promise about the Messiah (Jer 33:14-26)	133

- B. Ezekiel 134
  - 1. Messiah as the Tender Shoot (Eze 17:22-24) 135
  - 2. Messiah as the Rightful King (Eze 21:25-27) 136
  - 3. Messiah as the Good Shepherd (Eze 34:23-31) 137
  - 4. Messiah as the Great Unifier of the Nation (Eze 37:15-28) 138
- C. Daniel
  - 1. Messiah as the Son of Man (Dan 7:13-14) 140
  - 2. Messiah as the Anointed Ruler Who Will Come (Dan 8:24-27) 141
15. Postexilic Prophets 143
    - A. Haggai
      - 1. Messiah as Desire of all Nations (Hag 2:6-9) 143
    - B. Zechariah 144
      - 1. Messiah's Work as High Priest (Zech 3:8-10) 145
      - 2. Messiah as King-Priest: Ruler of Nations (Zech 6:9-15) 145
      - 3. Messiah as King (Zech 9:9-10) 147
      - 4. Messiah's Four Titles (Zech 10:4) 147
        - a. Cornerstone 148
        - b. Tent Peg 148
        - c. The Battle-Bow 148
        - d. Absolute Ruler 148
      - 5. Messiah as Rejected Good Shepherd (Zech 11:4-14) 149
      - 6. Messiah as the Pierced One (Zech 12:10) 150
      - 7. Messiah as Smitten Companion of the Lord (Zech 13:7) . 151
    - C. Malachi
      - 1. Messiah as Messenger of the Covenant (Mal 3:1) 152
      - 2. Messiah as Sun of Righteousness (Mal 4:2) 153

Conclusion 155

Notes 158

Bibliography 165

About the Author 167

PREFACE

Dr. Ron Hunter once told me his professor asked his class to create a gospel sermon based soley on the Old Testament. This book is a reflection of the good sense of that challenge. Christ is a part of the eternal uncreated Godhead. Man was the crown of God's creation, but having been given free moral agency, Adam and Eve chose to disobey God and lost their innocence; this was the original sin. From then on he was desperately in need of a Savior. The race was evil continually and would not have survived God's anger were it not for Noah and God's grace. From the beginning God has had a promise-plan for man's salvation. A Covenant-making God spoke to man from generation to generation from Adam to Noah to Abraham to Israel to Moses to David and through the prophets. He called forth Israel to bring the man Christ Jesus into the world – God With Us. Christ is the culmination-fulfillment of that promise-plan. There would be no redemption without Jesus. There would be no hope without His resurrection. There would be no new creation without the eternal God who loves us so.

Seeing the big picture, the complete revelation of the Bible, is so important to our faith! Of course, as Paul said, "Now we see through a glass darkly;" we know in part, but in the fulfilled Promise we will see Jesus Christ fully; "we will see Him as He is." This is the full revelation of God. For the time being our great hunger to know Him more fully draws us more deeply into His Book.

My motivation for writing this overview is not so much technical-theological as it is a desire to know and teach the big picture. While I have neither high degree nor lofty experience, I have always had an ability to assimilate enough detail to present meaningful generalization, to extrapolate, get to the point and to summarize a large amount of material into its essence. Initially the effort is quite personal in that I need to know and understand the full revelation of Jesus Christ as given in the Bible. Long-range it is evangelical in that people need to believe more fully in the Christ of their salvation. We who have been blessed with a deep faith derived from trust in God's Word should be freely giving our faith away. We should be telling the Good News of salvation. But, we have nothing to give except that which we have received from God. His revelation of Himself reveals how much He loves us as He lavishly directs His attention toward His bride, the Church. Reading this book about His BOOK is like a preparation for the Bridegroom, white dress, hair and make-up, paying attention to every detail, as we cast light on the revelation of the Messiah in the Old Testament: GOD WITH US.

I have divided this presentation into three categories:

 I. The Messiah in Type, That We May Understand
 II. The Messiah in Form, That We May See and
 III. The Messiah in Prophecy, That We May Believe

Christ is the theme of both Testaments of the Bible. In the Old He is presented in shadow, in the New in substance; in the Old in pictures, in the New in person; in the Old in type, in the New in truth; in the Old in ritual, in the New in reality; in the Old latent, in the New patent; in the Old prophesied, in the New present; in the Old implicitly revealed, in the New explicitly revealed. The Law presents a foundation for Christ, and that is a "downward look." The History gives a preparation for Christ, and that is an "outward look." The Poetry provides aspiration for Christ, and that is an "upward look." Prophecy provides an expectation for Christ, and that is a "forward look."[1] The New Testament does not so much present a new Christ as it does a fulfilled Christ.

Oh, there is a New Covenant as prophesied by Jeremiah 31:31-34 and confirmed by Hebrews 8:6-13, but it is best understood as the continuation of God's marvelous promise rather than a new dispensation. I am not a proponent of "replacement theology," whereby Israel is superseded by the church due to its failure to receive Christ. Zechariah spoke of a branch being cut off (Israel) and a new one (the Gentiles) grafted in. But for us, this is nothing to gloat about, for He also will graft the original branch back in one day. The church has always been a part of the promise-plan of God (viz. that Abraham would bring a blessing to the entire world). Christ has been the fulfillment of this promise. We must therefore more fully see Christ in the Old Testament from Adam through Malachi as a "promise-plan."

To understand the predictive element aright we must see it in the light of the other elements. Every fulfilled promise is a fulfilled prediction; but it is exceedingly important to look at it as a promise and not as a mere prediction.[2]

Jesus began with Moses and all the prophets as He taught the disciples on the road to Emmaus and as He expounded all the Scriptures the things concerning Himself (Luke 24:27). Jesus said, *"You search the Scriptures, for in them you think you have eternal life; and these are they which testify of Me* (John 5:39). Jesus Christ is the fulfillment of the Old Testament foundation, preparation and expectation, and He is the reason that we can "hold fast the confession of our hope without wavering. For He who promised is faithful" (Heb 10:19-23).

PART I – CHRIST IN TYPE: THAT WE MAY UNDERSTAND

Introduction

*...which are a shadow of things to come,
but the substance is of Christ* (Col 2:17)

In Part I we will see the extent to which God has gone in order to give us a "picture" of Jesus Christ from the beginning. We must realize that the Christian worldview has amazing internal unity and consistency thanks to the model presented in the law and ritual as designed by the Great Painter/Creator God. We are able to look at what at first appears to be random direction from God for separation, cleansing, worship and celebration, and see with marvelous clarity in type, the coming Christ.

A type is a form of analogy that can be found in the Bible just as in all great literature. Like all analogies, a type combines identity and difference. David and Christ were both given kingly power and rule. In spite of the vast differences between David's royalty and Christ's, there are points of formal identity that make the comparison meaningful. Yet it is just this degree of difference that makes biblical types distinctive.[3] With this in mind we look at the biblical record of lives who exhibit Christ-like attributes. The Bible gives us several such examples which in type look forward to the Messiah Jesus who was yet to come.

In archetype is displayed the amazing divine oversight of the God of the Bible. Themes are repeated and developed in Scripture. These begin to be recognized by those who enjoy reading God's Word. They include a rich portrait of Old Testament patterns, types and allusions which point to the Person and Work of Jesus Christ. Here we want to treat a sampling of those scriptures.

CHAPTER 1
THE COVENANT OF PIECES

Our first example of type can be found in Genesis Chapter 15 in the life of Abram who had been given a promise of land by God. But Abram would not see it; it would be his descendants who inherited the Promised Land. That was a tough thing for him because he was getting old and did not yet have a son. He merely assumed that the inheritance would go to his Damascene servant Eliezer. But God said *"This one shall not be your heir, but one who will come from your own body shall be your heir."* It is not so much that Abram did not believe God; in fact, the Scripture says *"he believed in the Lord, and He accounted it to him for righteousness."* Abram just wanted some reassurance. *"How will I know that I will inherit it?"* he asked. God was kind in granting this request.

In a ceremony strange to our modern Western minds, Yahweh instructed Abram to prepare various sacrificial animals dividing them into two pieces each. The half-carcasses would create two rows with an isle between where the two parties could walk. This preparation reflected the ancient Near East tradition of covenant between two men whereby each would take a written copy of the covenant made between them and walk between the two halves of the animal sacrifice in the blood which dripped from them. This "blood covenant" implied that if either broke this solemn agreement, he would pay for it with his life.

After this elaborate preparation by Abram and a day of protecting the sacrificial animals from the buzzards, heavy darkness fell around him and he fell asleep. While he slept God enacted the covenant alone. In Abram's dream he saw a smoking pot and a blazing torch which passed between the pieces. Jeremiah 34:18-20 makes clear God's reassurance to Abram of His promise both of a land and a progeny that would inherit the land. However, in this scene God alone took the pledge and by that essentially said that if there were failure to the terms of the covenant, He Himself would die alone. This is a powerful and vivid illustration of the price of redemption which was completed on the cross of Calvary nearly two thousand years later.[4] The answer is not fully revealed until God's darkness shrouds Calvary. There God the Son bears the curse of His own imprecation, not because He is guilty but because He takes the place of the guilty. Such is the final cost of God's oath of grace. It points to the day when God's pledge by His own life would be paid in blood.[5]

You were redeemed... with the precious blood of Christ, as of a lamb without blemish and without spot (1 Pet 1:18-19).

CHAPTER 2
SLAVERY IN EGYPT

Throughout the Bible the result of sin is portrayed as enslavement and death. Of course it is characterized by ignorance or foolishness, as doubt, as disobedience, rebellion and perversion. But the slavery of the Hebrews in Egypt is a type for our understanding of the wages of sin. Through Abraham his descendants were chosen by God to bring salvation to the world. How ironic it seems that they would first multiply into a large population as they occupied a foreign land. What were they doing there? The Bible traces the story to the sin of Joseph's brothers who had thrown him into a pit intending to kill him at first, then had thought twice and done something nearly as horrific by delivering him as human traffic for twenty shekels of silver to a band of Midianite merchants (who then sold him as a slave in Egypt). Joseph's character along with God's blessing eventually caused him to rise in Egypt as second in command only to Pharaoh.

not bad for a slave! God can lift us out of the misery of our former lives and bless us as He desires. But this is not the end of the story.

Here came Joseph's brothers looking for food during a drought in Canaan, the same brothers who had wished him dead. Who did they have to appeal to for food but the second in command in Egypt. God's ironies are not really ironies; they are His purview and His sovereignty at work. When Joseph finally revealed his true identity as their brother, his vile brothers rightly expected some sort of revenge or retribution. Instead Joseph wept, hugged and kissed his brothers as we will discuss ahead. As a Christ-type, Joseph offered redemption instead of punishment. Joseph's response was *"Do not be afraid; for am I in the place of God? But as for you, you meant evil against me; but God meant evil for good, in order to bring it about as it is this day, to save many people alive"* (Gen 50:19-20).

Joseph moved his father Jacob and the entire family to Egypt where ostensibly he could take care of them. It looked like a permanent move for God's chosen family. The descendants of Jacob thrived, and they grew into a tribe so huge they seemed a threat to Pharaoh. The result: 400 years of slavery.

The wages of the sin of Joseph's brothers had not yet been paid. This backdrop sets the stage for the big picture of redemption in the Exodus. But in it God clearly warns us of a principle that Jesus articulated, *"I tell you the truth, everyone who sins is a slave to sin"* (John 8:34).[6] This provides an archetype for the rest of Scripture: Slavery in Egypt is to be in the bondage of sin. Not only would this provide a reference for Exodus from the bondage of sin, but for the release provided by the blood of Christ from sin's slavery for all mankind. As with Joseph's brothers, a price would have to be paid. The blood sacrifice of the Lamb of God would bring freedom to an entire race, despite the ravages of sin.

CHAPTER 3
THE TABERNACLE

It is amazing that God desired to be present with the Israelites! He went to such elaborate effort to make that possible. Oh yes, there were covenants pre- and post-diluvian and there were unconditional promises made to Abraham: that of a great nation, a land and a blessing to the whole world. But, most interesting is the friendship that God had with Abraham. The Bible says that He believed God and that God accounted that to Abraham as righteousness. He was a friend of God! Their conversation seemed mostly direct as if Abraham experienced the frequent and personal presence of God. The theme reappears in Moses' relationship with God:

My Presence will go with you, and I will give you rest
(Exod 33:14).

The single most important fact in the experience of this new nation of Israel was that God had come to "tabernacle," or "dwell," in their midst.[7] Nowhere was this stated more clearly than in Exodus 29:42-46, where in connection with the tabernacle it was announced:

There [at the entrance] I will meet you and speak to you; there also I will meet with the Israelites, and the place will be consecrated by My glory. So I will consecrate the Tent of Meeting and the altar... I will dwell [tabernacle] among the Israelites and be their God. They will know that I am the Lord their God, who brought them out of Egypt so that I might dwell among them. I am the Lord their God.

This portable sanctuary was first erected under God's direction exactly one year after the Passover which freed the Israelites from Egyptian slavery. It traveled with the people and was set up wherever they pitched camp. The tabernacle would be in the center of the camp, and the 12 tribes of Israel would set up their tents around it according to tribe. In the above artist's conception we can envision God's design for sacrifice, cleansing and worship as set up by God's word to Moses on Mt. Sinai in Exodus Chapters 25-30.

> *They are to make a sanctuary for Me so that I may dwell among them. You must make it according to all that I show you – the pattern of the tabernacle as well as the pattern of all its furnishings* (Exod 25:8-9).

Fine white linen curtains embroidered with cherubim of blue, scarlet and purple surrounded the interior reminding one of the cherubim which surrounded Eden to prevent re-entry of Adam and Eve into the garden (Gen 3:24). But at the only doorway into the tabernacle there were no cherubim. It is hard to miss the significance that access to God's presence and to life is blocked except through God's only provision, a door. Jesus spoke of Himself as "the door," and the only access to the Father for the sake of atonement redemption (John 10:9; 14:6). Jesus taught us to *"enter through the narrow gate, for wide is the gate and broad is the road that leads to destruction, and many enter through it. But small is the gate and narrow the road that leads to life, and only a few find it"* (Matt 7:13-14).

The outer layers of "sea cow skins" are presumed to be a part of the Egyptian plunder and were probably the dugong which were very plentiful in the shallow waters on the shores of the Red Sea, a marine animal from 12 to 30 feet long, something between a whale and a seal, never leaving the water, but very easily caught. [9] Dr. Ronald Hunter sees these outer layers as unattractive, though water proof. But isn't that just as Isaiah told us in prophecy regarding Jesus Christ? [10]

He has no form or comeliness; And when we see Him, There is no beauty that we should desire Him (Isa 53:2).

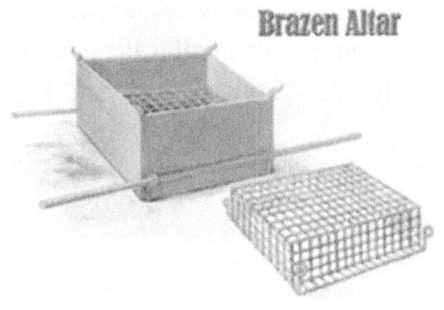
Brazen Altar

The Brazen Altar was the first thing one would see when entering the tabernacle. This altar of burnt offering made of acacia wood and bronze was to satisfy a moral principle in which there is no remission of sins except by the shedding of blood. The grace of God allowed a substitutionary sacrifice.

This foreshadows in type the atonement of the cross of Jesus who in His last words said "It is finished" (John 19:13). After Jesus' substitutionary sacrifice of His own blood, the repeated sacrifice by the high priests need not continue, for the sacrifice of the Son of God was perfect and final (Heb 7:22-28). God made him who had no sin to be sin for us, so that in Him we might become the righteousness of God (2 Cor 5:21)

Laver

Secondly, when entering the Tabernacle one would see the Lavar, a large basin for ceremonial washing (Exod 30:17-21). A worshiper must be clean in order to come into the presence of God. This dual act of preparation, the sacrifice and the cleansing, looks forward to the first and second works of grace as described in the New Testament.

> *If we confess our sins, He is faithful and righteous to forgive us our sins and to cleanse us from all unrighteousness* (1 John 1:9)
> *I baptize you with water for repentance, but the One who is coming after me is more powerful than I. I am not worthy to remove His sandals. He Himself will baptize you with the Holy Spirit and fire* (Matt 3:11).

> *Husbands, love your wives, just as Christ loved the church and gave Himself for her to make her holy, cleansing her with the washing of water by the word. He did this to present the church to Himself in splendor, without spot or wrinkle or anything like that, but holy and blameless* (Eph 5:26-27).

> *Draw near to God, and He will draw near to you. Cleanse your hands, sinners, and purify your hearts, double-minded people!* (James 4:8).

When the Samaritans had been baptized by Philip in the name of Jesus, they had not yet received the Holy Spirit. So, Peter and John were sent. They prayed for them, laid hands on them, and they received the Holy Spirit (Acts 8:14-17). Paul wrote to the church in Thessalonica, "We pray very earnestly night and day to see you face to face and to complete what is lacking in your faith" (1 Thes 3:10). Paul's desire for them was that "He may make [their] hearts blameless in holiness before our God" (3:13) and it was God's will to sanctify them (4:3). Paul closes his letter by saying, "Now may the God of peace Himself sanctify you completely. And may your spirit, soul, and body be kept sound and blameless for the coming of our Lord Jesus Christ" (5:23). Here is a cleansing away of original sin that the desire to sin be removed. We can hear Jesus' words to the woman taken in sin: "Neither do I condemn you; go and sin no more" (John 8:11). The ritual cleansing of the Tabernacle surely looked forward to God's intention to "cleanse us from all unrighteousness."

At one end of the Tabernacle lay out was located the Tent of Meeting or "Holy Place."

Sinless and cleansed the High Priest was then allowed to enter into this Sanctuary where there were positioned three important furnishings:

The menorah, also called the "golden lampstand" or "candlestick," stood at the left side of the Holy Place. It was hammered out of one piece of pure gold as with the laver, there were no specific instructions about the size of the menorah, but the fact that it was fashioned out of one piece of pure gold would have limited its size.

The lampstand had a central branch from which three branches extended from each side, forming a total of seven branches. Seven lamps holding olive oil and wicks stood on top of the branches. Each branch looked like that of an almond tree, containing buds, blossoms and flowers.

The priests were instructed to keep the lamps burning continuously. The lampstand was the only source of light in the Holy Place, so without it, the priests would have been groping around in the dark. The light shone upon the table of showbread and the altar of incense enabled the priests to fellowship with God and intercede on behalf of God's people. Just as the lampstand was placed in God's dwelling place so that the priests could approach God, Jesus, the "true light that gives light to every man" (John 1:9) came into the world so that man could see God and not live in spiritual darkness anymore. Jesus said:

"I am the light of the world. Whoever follows me will never walk in darkness, but will have the light of life." (John 8:12)

"I have come into the world as a light, so that no one who believes in me should stay in darkness." (John 9:46)

Jesus is represented by the main branch of the lampstand, and we as believers are represented by the six branches that extend from the original branch. Having believed, we are now living as "children of light" (Ephesians 5:8) who draw our source of light from Jesus, the true light. Jesus calls us the "light of the world" and commands us to "let your light shine before men, that they may see your good deeds and praise your Father in heaven" (Matthew 5:14,16). The branches of the menorah serve as a picture of Jesus' description of our relationship with him: "I am the vine, you are the branches ... apart from me you can do nothing" *(John 15:5).*

Two other significant facts that can be seen are that it was made of *pure gold* (not gold plated) and had *seven* branches. Pure gold is a representation of the deity and perfection of Jesus Christ, and seven is the number of completeness in the Bible. The believer is made *complete* by the *perfection* of Christ.

The table of showbread was a small table made of acacia wood and overlaid with pure gold. It measured 3 feet by 1.5 feet and was 2 feet, 3 inches high. It stood on the right side of the Holy Place across from the lampstand and held 12 loaves of bread, representing the 12 tribes of Israel. The priests baked the bread with fine flour and it remained on the table before the Lord for a week; every Sabbath day the priests would remove it and eat it in the Holy Place, then put fresh bread on the table. Only priests could eat the bread, and it could only be eaten in the Holy Place, because it was holy.

"Showbread" also was called "bread of the presence" because it was to be always in the Lord's presence. The table and the bread were a picture of God's willingness to have fellowship and communion (literally speaking, sharing something in common) with man. It was like an invitation to share a meal, an extension of friendship. Eating together often is an act of fellowship. God was willing for man to enter into His presence to fellowship with Him, and this invitation was always open. Jesus exemplified this when He ate with tax collectors, prostitutes and the sinners of Jewish society. But this was more than just a gesture of friendship on earth. Jesus came to call sinners to Him, make them right with God, so that they could enjoy everlasting fellowship with God.

> *"I am the bread of life. He who comes to me will never go hungry, and he who believes in me will never be thirsty. ... Your forefathers ate the manna in the desert, yet they died. But here is the bread that comes down from heaven, which a man may eat and not die." (John 6:35, 49-50)*

God so desires our fellowship that He was willing to come to earth from heaven as our "bread of life" to give eternal life to all those who would partake in it. At Jesus' last Passover meal with His disciples, Jesus described Himself as bread again:

> *"While they were eating, Jesus took bread, gave thanks and broke it, and gave it to his disciples, saying, 'Take and eat; this is my body.'" (Matthew 26:26)*

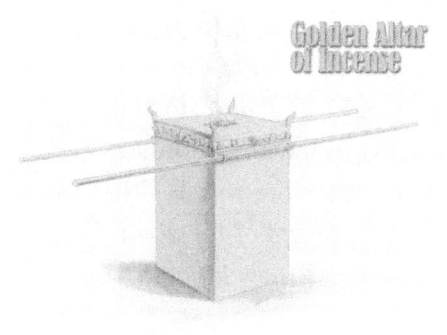
Golden Altar of Incense

The golden altar of incense, which is not to be confused with the brazen altar, sat in front of the curtain that separated the Holy Place from the Holy of Holies. This altar was smaller than the brazen altar. It was a square with each side measuring 1.5 feet and was 3 feet high. It was made of acacia wood and overlaid with pure gold. Four horns protruded from the four corners of the altar. God commanded the priests to burn incense on the golden altar every morning and evening at the same time that the daily burnt offerings were made. The incense was to be left burning continually throughout the day and night as a pleasing aroma to the Lord. It was made of an equal part of four precious spices (stacte, onycha, galbanum and frankincense) and was considered holy.

God commanded the Israelites not to use the same formula outside the tabernacle to make perfume for their own consumption; otherwise, they were to be cut off from their people (Exodus 30:34-38). The incense was a symbol of the prayers and intercession of the people going up to God as a sweet fragrance. God wanted His dwelling to be a place where people could approach Him and pray to Him.

"...for my house will be called a house of prayer for all nations." (Isaiah 56:7)

"May my prayer be set before you like incense; may the lifting up of my hands be like the evening sacrifice." (Psalm 141:2)

The picture of prayers wafting up to heaven like incense is captured in David's psalm and also in John's vision in Revelation:

"Another angel, who had a golden censer, came and stood at the altar. He was given much incense to offer, with the prayers of all the saints, on the golden altar before the throne. The smoke of the incense, together with the prayers of the saints, went up before God from the angel's hand." (Revelation 8:3-4)

The golden altar, furthermore, is a representation of Christ, who is our intercessor before God the Father. During His days on earth, Jesus prayed for the believers. He was like the high priest of the tabernacle, who bore the names of each of the Israelite tribes on his breastplate before God. Just before He was betrayed and sentenced to death, Jesus interceded for His disciples and all believers, asking God to guard them from evil and sanctify them by His Word, and that they may see God's glory and be a witness to the world (John 17:1-26). Today, Jesus still is our high priest at the Father's side, interceding for God's people:

> "Christ Jesus, who died — more than that, who was raised to life — is at the right hand of God and is also interceding for us." (Romans 8:34)

Since we have been forgiven of our sins through the blood of Christ, we also come boldly in prayer in Jesus' name. When we pray in Jesus' name, we are praying based on the work He has done and not on our own merit. It is in His powerful name that we are saved and baptized, and in His name we live, speak and act.

> "And I will do whatever you ask in my name, so that the Son may bring glory to the Father. You may ask me for anything in my name, and I will do it." (John 14:13-14)

The horns of the golden altar were sprinkled with blood from the animal sacrifice to cleanse and purify it from the sins of the Israelites (Leviticus 4:7, 16:18). Just as the horns on the brazen altar represent the power of Christ's blood to forgive sins, the horns on the golden altar signify the power of His blood in prayer as we confess our sins and ask for His forgiveness.

Within the Holy Place of the tabernacle, there was an inner room called the Holy of Holies, or the Most Holy Place. Judging from its name, we can see that it was a most sacred room, a place no ordinary person could enter. It was God's special dwelling place in the midst of His people.

During the Israelites' wanderings in the wilderness, God appeared as a pillar of cloud or fire in and above the Holy of Holies. The Holy of Holies was a perfect cube — its length, width and height were all equal to 15 feet.

A thick curtain separated the Holy of Holies from the Holy Place. This curtain, known as the "veil," was made of fine linen and blue, purple and scarlet yarn. There were figures of cherubim (angels) embroidered onto it. Cherubim, spirits who serve God, were in the presence of God to demonstrate His almighty power and majesty. They also guarded the throne of God. These cherubim were also on the innermost layer of the covering of the tent. If one looked upward, they would see the cherubim figures.

The word "veil" in Hebrew means a screen, divider or separator that hides. What was this curtain hiding? Essentially, it was shielding a holy God from sinful man. Whoever entered into the Holy of Holies was entering the very presence of God. In fact, anyone except the high priest who entered the Holy of Holies would die. Even the high priest, God's chosen mediator with His people, could only pass

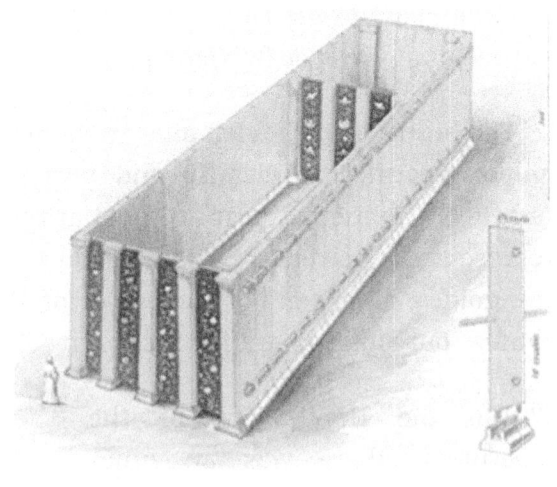

through the veil and enter this sacred dwelling once a year, on a prescribed day called the Day of Atonement.

The picture of the veil was that of a barrier between man and God, showing man that the holiness of God could not be trifled with. God's eyes are too pure to look on evil and He can tolerate no sin (Habakkuk 1:13). The veil was a barrier to make sure that man could not carelessly and irreverently enter into God's awesome presence. Even as the high priest entered the Holy of Holies on the Day of Atonement, he had to make some meticulous preparations: He had to wash himself, put on special clothing, bring burning incense to let the smoke cover his eyes from a direct view of God, and bring blood with him to make atonement for sins.

> *"But only the high priest entered the inner room, and that only once a year, and never without blood, which he offered for himself and for the sins the people had committed in ignorance."* (Hebrews 9:7)

So the presence of God remained shielded from man behind a thick curtain during the history of Israel. However, Jesus' sacrificial death on the cross changed that. When He died, the curtain in the Jerusalem temple was torn in half, from the top to the bottom. Only God could have carried out such an incredible feat because the veil was too high for human hands to have reached it, and too thick to have torn it. (The Jerusalem temple, a replica of the wilderness tabernacle, had a curtain that was about 60 feet in height, 30 feet in width and four inches thick.) Furthermore, it was torn from top down, meaning this act must have come from above. As the veil was torn, the Holy of Holies was exposed. God's presence was now accessible to all. Shocking as this may have been to the priests ministering in the temple that day, it is indeed good news to us as believers, because we know that Jesus' death has atoned for our sins and made us right before God. The torn veil illustrated Jesus' body broken for us, opening the way for us to come to God. As Jesus cried out "It is finished!" on the cross, He was indeed proclaiming that God's redemptive plan was now complete. The age of animal offerings was over. The ultimate offering had been sacrificed. We can now boldly enter into God's presence, "the inner sanctuary behind the curtain, where Jesus, who went before us, has entered on our behalf." (Hebrews 6:19-20)

> *"Therefore, brothers, since we have confidence to enter the Most Holy Place by the blood of Jesus, by a new and living way opened for us through the curtain, that is, his body ...let us draw near to God with a sincere heart in full assurance of faith." (Hebrews 10:19-22)*

The Holy of Holies is a representation of heaven itself, God's dwelling place, to which we now have access through Christ. In Revelation, John's vision of heaven — the New Jerusalem — also was a perfect square, just as the Holy of Holies was (Revelation 21:16).

> *"For Christ did not enter a man-made sanctuary that was only a copy of the true one; he entered heaven itself, now to appear for us in God's presence. Nor did he enter heaven to offer himself again and again, the way the high priest enters the Most Holy Place every year with blood that is not his own. ...But now he has appeared once for all at the end of the ages to do away with sin by the sacrifice of Himself." (Hebrews 9:24-26)*

Within the Holy of Holies, shielded from the eye of the common man, was one piece of furniture comprising two parts:

the Ark of the Covenant and the atonement cover (or "mercy seat") on top of it. The ark was a chest made of acacia wood, overlaid with pure gold inside and out. It was 3 feet, 9 inches long and 2 feet, 3 inches wide and high.

God commanded Moses to put in the ark three items: a golden pot of manna, Aaron's staff that had budded, and the two stone tablets on which the Ten Commandments were written. We will discuss these three objects in further detail below.

The atonement cover was the lid for the ark. On top of this "Mercy Seat" stood two cherubim (angels) at the two ends, facing each other. The cherubim, symbols of God's divine presence and power, were facing downward toward the ark with outstretched wings that covered the atonement cover. The whole structure was beaten out of one piece of pure gold. The atonement cover was God's dwelling place in the tabernacle. It was His throne, flanked by angels. God said to Moses:

> *"There, above the cover between the two cherubim that are over the ark of the Testimony, I will meet with you and give you all my commands for the Israelites." (Exodus 25:22)*

> *"Tell your brother Aaron not to come whenever he chooses into the Most Holy Place behind the curtain in front of the atonement cover on the ark, or else he will die, because I appear in the cloud over the atonement cover." (Leviticus 16:2)*

Other Scriptures also speak of God's throne:

> *"...the ark of God, which is called by the Name, the name of the Lord Almighty, who is enthroned between the cherubim that are on the ark." (2 Samuel 6:2)*

> *"O Lord Almighty, God of Israel, enthroned between the cherubim, you alone are God over all the kingdoms of the earth." (Isaiah 37:16)*

Above the ark and the atonement cover, God appeared in His glory in "unapproachable light" (1 Timothy 6:16). This light is sometimes referred to as the Shekinah glory. The word *Shekinah*, although it does not appear in our English bibles, has the same roots as the word for *tabernacle* in Hebrew and refers to the *presence of the Lord*.

Because the ark was God's throne among His people, it was a symbol of His presence and power with them wherever it went. There are quite a number of miracles recorded in the Old Testament surrounding the ark: With the presence of the ark, the waters of the River Jordan divided so the Israelites could cross on dry land, and the walls of Jericho fell so that the Israelites could capture it (Joshua 3:14-17, 6:6-21). Yet the ark could not be treated with irreverence because it was also a symbol of God's judgment and wrath. When the Israelites fought their enemies the Philistines during the time of the prophet Samuel, they disregarded the commands of the Lord and took the ark out to the battlefield with them, "summoning" God's presence. God caused the Philistines to win the battle and "the glory departed from Israel, for the ark of the Lord was taken" (1 Samuel 4:22). However, God showed His power to the Philistines when He caused their idol, Dagon, to fall to the ground when the ark was placed next to it, and several Philistine cities were plagued heavily when the ark was in their midst (1 Samuel 5). Ultimately, the ark was returned to Israel.

What may seem strange to us today is that, hidden in the special golden box representing God's presence were not treasures and precious gems, but three unlikely items: a jar of bread, a stick and two stones. What were these curious keepsakes and why did God want them in His ark? The three articles represented some of the most embarrassing and disgraceful events in the history of the Israelites.

First, the pot of manna:

> "This is what the Lord has commanded: 'Take an omer [portion for one man] of manna and keep it for the generations to come, so they can see the bread I gave you to eat in the desert when I brought you out of Egypt.'" (Exodus 16:32)

God had provided this bread-like food for the Israelites when they grumbled during the wanderings in the desert. It was bread from heaven! He continued to provide the food daily and faithfully, but the people were not one bit thankful. They complained and wanted something else. The pot of manna was an uncomfortable reminder that despite what God had provided for them, the Israelites had rejected God's provision.

Second, Aaron's staff that had budded: The people, out of jealousy, rebelled against Aaron as their high priest. To resolve the dispute, God commanded the people to take 12 sticks written with the names of the leader of each tribe and place them before the ark overnight. The next day, Aaron's rod from the house of Levi had budded with blossoms and almonds. God confirmed his choice of Aaron's household as the priestly line.

> *"And the Lord said to Moses, 'Put back the staff of Aaron before the testimony, to be kept as a sign for the rebels, that you may make an end of their grumblings against me, lest they die.'" (Numbers 17:10)*

The staff reminded the Israelites that on more than one occasion, they had rejected God's authority.

Third, the two stone tablets with the Ten Commandments: God had chosen the Israelites as His special people. For the Israelites to qualify for that distinction, God had demanded one thing. They must obey His Law, the Ten Commandments. This was a conditional agreement:

> *"Now if you obey me fully and keep my covenant, then out of all nations you will be my treasured possession. Although the whole earth is mine, you will be for me a kingdom of priests and a holy nation." (Exodus 19:5-6)*

The Israelites had said heartily, "All that the Lord has spoken we will do," in response to God's covenant (Exod 19:8). But how did they fare in fulfilling their end of the contract? Miserably. It was impossible for them to keep the Ten Commandments perfectly. Over and over again, they violated God's holy Law, and God made it clear to them the consequences of their sin by sending plagues, natural hazards and foreign armies upon them. The stone tablets in the ark were a reminder that the Israelites had rejected God's right standard of living.

These three articles were preserved in the ark throughout Israel's history as an unpleasant symbol of man's sins and shortcomings, a reminder of how they rejected God's provision, authority and right standard of living. It pointed to man as a helpless sinner. It may have been uncomfortable to think that God's splendor was so close to the three articles associated with man's sinfulness. But this is where God's provision comes in. When God looked down from His presence above the ark, He did not see the reminders of sin. They were covered by a necessary object — the atonement cover.

Every year, the high priest would enter the Holy of Holies on the Day of Atonement. Bringing burning incense to shield his eyes from a direct view of God's glory, he sprinkled blood from a bull onto the atonement cover for his and his household's sins, then sprinkled blood from a goat for all the sins of Israel. God promised that when He saw the blood, it would cover over man's sin. (To *atone for* means to *cover* — hence the name *atonement cover*.) God did not see the sin anymore but the provision instead, and it appeased His wrath. The Israelites found acceptance with God by believing His word to be true — that when their sins were covered by blood, God temporarily overlooked their sins as if they had been obliterated. But Jesus Christ has become *our* permanent atonement cover. Through Jesus' blood, our sins have been covered. When God looks at us, He doesn't see our sin, but the provision: His own Son. Jesus lay down His life for us as an innocent sacrifice so that God would look on us and see His perfection. The atonement cover was God's throne in the midst of the Israelites. God is on His throne today in heaven, and Jesus, our high priest, is at His right hand. Approaching His throne is approaching the throne of grace.

> *"Let us then approach the throne of grace with confidence, so that we may receive mercy and find grace to help us in our time of need."* (Heb 4:16)

The three items in the ark that served as a sore reminder of man's shortcomings have taken on a different meaning since Jesus Christ redeemed us from our sins. Let's review the three articles and see how they point to Christ.

<u>Consider the pot of manna</u>: When Jesus came and walked on earth, he didn't reject God's provision. Rather, He became God's provision to us. Manna, the bread from heaven, in itself did not impart life. But Jesus told us that He is the true bread from heaven.

> *Jesus said to them, 'I tell you the truth, it is not Moses who has given you the bread from heaven, but it is my Father who gives you the true bread from heaven. I am the bread of life. Your forefathers ate the manna in the desert, yet they died. But here is the bread that comes down from heaven, which a man may eat and not die.'" (John 6:32, 48-50)*

<u>Secondly, Aaron's budding staff</u>: Jesus didn't reject God's authority. Instead, He submitted Himself to the Father's will and died on the cross.

> *"For I have come down from heaven not to do my will but to do the will of him who sent me." (John 6:38)*

> *But He came back to life like Aaron's budding rod, "the firstfruits from the dead" (1 Cor 15:20).*

> *"I am the resurrection and the life. He who believes in me will live, even though he dies; and whoever lives and believes in me will never die." (John 11:15-26)*

Thirdly, the Ten Commandments: Jesus didn't reject God's right standard of living. He lived a sinless life and obeyed God's law perfectly, becoming our perfect sacrifice and intercessor. His sacrifice instituted a new covenant that was not based on the Law. [11]

> *But now a righteousness from God, apart from law, has been made known, to which the Law and the Prophets testify. This righteousness from God comes through faith in Jesus Christ to all who believe* (Rom 3:20-22).

CHAPTER 4
THE PASSOVER AND DAY OF ATONEMENT

I remember having a gentleman from Jews for Jesus come to our church a couple of times and in a display of show-and-tell demonstrate the significance of the elements of the Passover meal as it pointed toward Jesus Christ. It is called "Seder" because it involves a retelling of the story of the liberation of the Israelites from slavery in ancient Egypt. Jesus had been fervently desiring to eat this Passover meal with His disciples before He suffered (Luke 22:15). We usually designate this meal as "the last supper." From the ritual of the Seder we derive the sacrament of communion. Jesus said, "Do this in remembrance of Me" (Luke 22:19). It was interesting, but I did not pay attention so as to memorize the detail. Nevertheless, I have been aware for many years that there was significant and pointed, non-incidental and purposeful metaphor that caused a forward look important to Christians and Jews alike. It presents not only a story of deliverance from slavery in Egypt, it tells a story of Redemption:

Sea-soaked karpas and the bitter herb remind the Jew of the tears shed in slavery under Pharaoh's thumb, a reminder that life in bondage without redemption is a life drowned in tears. The Passover lamb points to the God of Israel who in his unwavering commitment to deliverance reigned down plagues on Pharaoh's Egypt. The worst of these came in the darkness of death's shadow. But God's outstretched arm shielded the Hebrews from harm giving one narrow way to escape through the covering of each door with the blood of a spotless lamb. This, the one measure of obedience meant to save every first-born son, a sacrifice in blood. It was by the sacrifice that freedom was secured. Death passed over the blood-painted door posts. They were spared a swift judgement and delivered from Pharaoh because of the blood of a lamb. Heeding a warning from God that Pharaoh would pursue the Israelites in their exodus, the Israelites took with them unleavened bread. And so, with Passover, leaven is removed from the home and the heart since leaven is a reminder of the past and of sin. So why should we dwell on such a story? Perhaps because our own often self-serving choices can once again enslave us making us deaf to the voice of the One who wants us to experience true freedom. Only He can deliver us from the delusion that we know best. Without Him we are as alone as the Israelites in the desert of Egypt. Only by crying out to the God of Israel and accepting his sovereignty can our bondage be broken. The Passover Jesus shared with His disciples at the Last Supper signaled the end of blood sacrifice. He paid the ultimate price when He died at Calvary. As the Son of God, He came to deliver us from more than just the slavery of Pharaoh but from our own sin so that death will pass us over. Jesus is the Lamb of God, broken, buried and brought back. He is the Sacrificial Lamb, the blood on the doorpost of our hearts. And, by His death and resurrection He brands us, all of us, free, forgiven and loved. [12]

Of course, the archetypal or word pictures presented of the coming Messiah are recognized more fully because of such prophetic passages as Isaiah 49:3-13. The Messiah will be a servant who will bring Israel to God and be a light for the nations. Isaiah 53:3-12 reveals that He will bear our sorrows, our griefs, be wounded for our iniquities, be bruised for our transgressions, and by whose stripes we will be healed. He would be like a lamb led to slaughter, and yet resurrected. Through this prophecy we are able to see types and images of Christ in the sacrificial system, especially the Passover and Day of Atonement.[13]

The shophar (trumpet) was a ceremonial ram's horn used to call the people of Israel together (Exod 19:16). The shophar was to be blown on the Day of Atonement in the Jubilee Year to signal the release of slaves and debt. It also was used as a trumpet of war as Israelites were campaigning against their enemies. As such it is an instrument of warning and announcement. In the New Testament the trumpet is a key signal for the Second Coming of Christ (Mat 24:31); 1 Cor 15:51-52; 1 Thes 4:16; Rev 8:13).

The Day of Atonement (Yom kippur) is the holiest day of the Jewish year, and provides prophetic insight regarding the Second coming of the Messiah, the restoration of national Israel, and the final judgment of the world. It is also a day that reveals the work of Yeshua as our High Priest after the order of Melchizedek (Gen 14:17-20; Heb 5:10; 6:20). Leviticus 16:29 mandates this holy day on the 10th day of the 7th month as the Day of Atonement for sins. Leviticus 23:27 decrees that Yom Kippur is a strict day of rest. The Day of Atonement was the climax of the Old Testament sacrificial system displaying the holiness of God and the depth of humanity's sin. But God is merciful and gracious, slow to anger, and abounding in steadfast love and faithfulness, keeping steadfast love for thousands, forgiving iniquity and transgression and sin (Exod 34:6).

One of the unique elements about the Day of Atonement was the role of the scapegoat. The high priest was instructed to take two goats, and lots were cast to determine which goat was to be slaughtered and which was to be cast out into the wilderness. After the first goat was slaughtered, the high priest laid both hands on the head of the second goat. He confessed all the sins of Israel over it, and then the scapegoat was cast out of the camp and into the wilderness. The sanctuary was cleansed; the sacrifice was offered to pay the penalty for the people; and now the sins of the people were symbolically carried away (Lev 16:7-10). The scapegoat never returned and likely died in the wilderness. **Psalm 103:11-12** says that God is so loving that for those who trust in Him, He removes our sin and transgression as far as the east is from the west. The scapegoat highlights theologically man's need for expiation, the removal of guilt and impurity.

The Fall left humanity with two grave problems. Because of sin, men and women are guilty before a holy God and deserving of God's wrath and punishment, and humanity became polluted with the taint of sin. The Day of Atonement both caused God to turn away His wrath and cancelled the sin of God's covenant people, the sacrificial goat paying the price of death in place of God's people and the scapegoat removing the tarnishing effects of sin.

> *For the wages of sin is death, but the free gift of God is eternal life in Christ Jesus our Lord* (Rom 6:23).

Yom Kippur was a temporary, partial solution until the fullness of time had come. The Day of Atonement was a foreshadowing of Jesus Christ, the Lamb of God who took away the sin of the world. The high priest, the slaughtered goat and the scapegoat were shadows to point to the ultimate Day of Atonement when Jesus Christ offered Himself as a sacrifice for us on the cross. Jesus is the Great High Priest who offered on behalf of His people the perfect once for all sacrifice, the Slaughtered Lamb whose blood was poured to pay the penalty of death and the Scapegoat who died outside the city taking **away the sin of the world (Heb. 7:27; 9:12,26,28; 10:10; 13:12). Jesus the perfect, spotless and precious Lamb, who knew no sin, God made to be sin for us (2 Cor. 5:21).**[14]

CHAPTER 5
THE FEAST OF TABERNACLES

The fourth annual festival of those regular religious celebrations remembering God's great acts of salvation in the history of Israel is called the Feast of Tabernacles (or Booths). Along with the Passover Feast and the Feast of Pentecost, the Feast of Tabernacles required the attendance of Jewish males living within twenty miles of Jerusalem. The dwelling in booths or "tabernacles" for a seven-day period is meant to be a joyful reminder of the protection, preservation and shelter from heat and storm. The observance of this feast combined the ingathering of the labor of the field, the ingathering of the threshing floor and winepress and the dwelling in booths (which reflected the dwelling in such booths after their exodus from Egypt). After the return from exile, Ezra read the law and led the people in acts of penitence during this feast (Neh 8:13-9:3).

Later additions to the ritual included a libation of water drawn from the pool of Siloam (the probable background for Jesus' comments on "living water," John 7:37-39) and the lighting of huge menorahs (candelabra) at the Court of the Women (the probable background for Jesus' statement, "I am the light of the world," John 8:12 HCSB). The water and the "pillar of light" provided during the wilderness wandering (when the people dwelt in tabernacles) was temporary and in contrast to the continuing water and light claimed by Jesus during this feast which commemorated that wandering period.

Water:

By the time of Christ a daily ritual had become the custom involving a march around the great altar and then down to the pool of Siloam. The priests would carry along a golden pitcher with which to draw water from the pool and then bring the filled pitcher back up to the Temple. On their way back through the Water Gate, the people would recite the words of the prophet Isaiah 12:3. The words are memorialized in the chorus:

> *Therefore with joy shall ye draw water*
> *Out of the wells of salvation*
> *And in that day shall ye say, "Praise the Lord."*[15]

Once back at the Temple, the water from the golden pitcher would be poured out on the great altar as an offering to God. All the while the people would sing the Hallel (Psalms 113-118). This was a thanksgiving for the gift of water, and enacted prayer for rain and a memorial of the event in the Exodus when water sprang from the rock at Horeb.[16]

When Jesus talked to the Samaritan woman at Jacob's well, He told her:

> *"If you knew the gift of God, and who it is who says to you, 'Give Me a drink,' you would have asked Him, and He would have given you living water"* (John 4:10).

The apostle Paul made the Messianic connection for us when he wrote:
> *...and all drank the same spiritual drink. For they drank of that spiritual Rock that followed them, and that Rock was Christ* (1 Cor 10:4).

Jesus had revealed the significance of this archetype when at the last day of the Feast of Tabernacles He cried out saying,

> *"If anyone thirst, let him come to Me and drink. He who believes in Me, as the Scripture has said, out of his heart will flow rivers of living water"* (John 7:37b-38).

John went on to explain, *"But this He spoke concerning the Spirit, whom those believing in Him would receive"* (John 7:39).

The lighting of huge menorahs at the Court of the Women is probable background for Jesus' statement, *"I am the light of the world. He who follows Me shall not walk in darkness, but have the light of life"* (John 8:12). The water and the "pillar of fire" provided during the wilderness wandering (when people dwelt in tabernacles) was temporary and in contrast to the continuing water and light claimed by Jesus during this feast which commemorated that wandering period.

CHAPTER 6
THE THEME OF "FIRSTBORN" IN THE BIBLE

"FIRST BORN" represents a biblical archetype appearing as a golden thread throughout Scripture. The concept is important to biblical theology and understanding.
- It finds its significance in the Passover of Israel's firstborn in Egypt.
- It appears in the Law of Moses as special requirements and responsibilities of a couple's firstborn son.
- However, the archetype is expressed in the tithe or first-fruits of ones increase.
- It is expressed in the requirement to bring the firstborn of a clean animal to the sanctuary.
- It is expressed in Jesus Christ as the "firstborn among many brothers" (incarnation)
- and the "first born from the dead" (resurrection).

- Figuratively Israel is God's firstborn.
- Within Israel the tribe of Levi was its firstborn, sanctified for service to God.
- Finally, it is expressed with regard to every believer as "firstborn of those whose names are written in heaven."

The First Son Born: In ancient Israel the firstborn son of a newly married people was believed to represent the prime of human vigor (Gen 49:3; Psa 78:51; 105:36). Culturally, in the ancient Near East the birthright of a firstborn included a double portion of the estate and leadership of the family. In the succession of prophets, Elisha asked Elijah for a "double portion" of his spirit, an obvious allusion to the double portion of inheritance (2 Kings 2:9). As head of the house after his father's death, the eldest son customarily cared for his mother until her death, and he also provided for his sisters until their marriage. The firstborn might sell his rights as Esau did (Gen 25:29-34; Rom 9:12-13) or forfeit them for misconduct as Reuben did because of incest (Gen 35:22; 49:3-4; 1 Chron 5:1-2). Also, God in His sovereignty could override tradition in his selection of "firstborn" leadership: Isaac over Ishmael, Jacob over Esau, Ephraim before Manasseh and both before Reuben and Simeon, David over his older brothers (Psa 89:27) and Solomon over his older brother Adonijah (1 Kings 1-2).

Abraham in obedience offered up his firstborn son Isaac as a burnt offering to God, but God stayed his hand and provided a substitutionary ram as redemption for Isaac. Only those serving false gods actually sacrificed their babies to appease their gods. Child sacrifice was made to the Ammonite god, Molech (2 Kings 23:10). The misguided king of Moab offered his firstborn son as a burnt offering in order to find favor with his god because he could not prevail against Israel. The sacrifice of his son was successful; the prevailing over Israel was not (2 Kings 3:27).

Special Privilege and Responsibility: In the Law of Moses the first son born to a couple was required to be specially dedicated to God. In memory of the death of Egypt's firstborn and the preservation of the firstborn of Israel in the Passover, all the firstborn of Israel, both of man and beast, belonged to Yahweh (Exod 13:1-16; 22:29-30; 34:20; Num 3:13). This meant that the people of Israel attached unusual value to the eldest son and assigned special privileges and responsibilities to him. He was presented to the Lord when he was a month old. Joseph and Mary brought Jesus to the temple to fulfill the requirement of the firstborn (Luke 2:22-23).

Redemption: Since he belonged to the Lord, it was necessary for the father to buy back the child from the priest at a redemption price not to exceed five shekels [2 ounces of silver] (Num 18:16). The husband of several wives would have to redeem the firstborn of each.

Animal Sacrifice: Foreshadowing Moses, Abel brought the firstborn of his flock to the Lord (Gen 4:4). In the Levitical sacrificial system the firstborn of a clean animal was brought into the sanctuary on the eighth day after birth (Exod 22:29-30). If it were without blemish, it was sacrificed (Deut 15:19; Num 18:17). If it had a blemish, the priest to whom it was given could eat it as common food outside Jerusalem (Deut 15:21-23), or it could be eaten at home by its owner. Apparently the firstborn of a clean animal was not to be used for any work since it belonged to the Lord (Deut 15:19). The firstborn of an unclean animal had to be redeemed by an estimation of the priest, with the addition of one-fifth (Lev 27:27; Num 18:15). According to Exod 13:13; 34:20, the firstborn of an ass was either ransomed by a sheep or lamb, or its neck had to be broken.

Firstfruits: The Israelites were to bring a sheaf of the firstfruits of their harvest to the priest (Lev 23:10). Honoring the Lord with the firstfruits of their increase was required (Prov 3:9); withholding tithes and offerings was considered to be "robbing God" and a great blessing was attached to faithfulness in tithing (Malachi 3:8-10).

Israel, God's Firstborn: Figuratively, Israel was God's "firstborn" (Exod 4:22; Jer 31:9) and enjoyed priority status. God compared His relationship to Israel with the relationship of a father and his firstborn son. Within Israel, the tribe of Levi represented the firstborn of the nation in its worship ceremony (Num 3:40-41; 8:18).

Christ, the Firstborn: Christ is the "firstborn" of the Father (Heb 1:6) by having preeminent position over others in relation to Him. He is also described as "firstborn among many brothers" (Rom 8:29) and "firstborn over all creation" (Col 1:15). Paul (Col 1:18) and John (Rev 1:5) refer to Christ as "firstborn from the dead" – the first to rise bodily from the grave and not die again (1 Cor 15:20-23).

The Assembly of the Firstborn: Heb 12:23 refers to the "assembly of the firstborn whose names have been written in heaven". Christian believers, united as joint heirs with Christ, enjoy the status of "firstborn" in God's household. "He brought us forth by the word of truth, that we might be a kind of firstfruits of His creatures." (James 1:18) And we eagerly await the redemption of our body having "the firstfruits of the Spirit" (Rom 8:23).

The firstborn/firstfruits theme established with Moses continuously reminds the believer of his opportunity to give God his first and his best. The theme inspires parenthood and influences our sense of family responsibility. It leads us to tithe from our increase. It encourages us to put God first among all of our involvements. It tells us of the privilege of sanctification, to be set aside for service to the Lord. Finally, we are heirs and joint heirs with Christ who died for us, shed his blood for remission of our sin and has raised us up to *"Mount Zion and to the city of the living God, the heavenly Jerusalem, to an innumerable company of angels, to the general assembly and church of the firstborn who are registered in heaven, to God the Judge of all, to the spirits of just men made perfect, to Jesus the Mediator of the new covenant, and to the blood of sprinkling that speaks better things than that of Abel"* (Heb 12:22-24).

CHAPTER 7
THE LIVES OF CHRIST-LIKE MEN

Long before I experienced any depth of understanding about the Person of Jesus Christ, and therefore of the character and image of God, I had before me a witness and example, my own dad. Oakley Ethington was saved and sanctified wholly in the Salvation Army at age 17. I cannot walk by one of those famous red kettles without dropping a dollar in because I am so grateful for the example of my dad. He was confident and secure not only in his salvation but that God had purified his heart. And, his life showed it. There was a sweetness about him that I seldom see in people. There was a consistency of character in him. He wasn't much of a disciplinarian, although we got spanked. We knew that if we did something like lie, cheat or steal, that my dad would be grieved. When I was 11 or 12 my brother and I went on a petty theft spree. We found we could go into retail stores, slyly drop things into our pockets and not have to pay for them. I had pens, knives, fishing lures, candy and much I can't even remember. I would throw those things into my bottom dresser drawer where my parents never saw. One day, overcome by guilt, I gathered the whole cache and threw it into the trash can. Wouldn't you know my dad soon took the trash out and spotted my booty. "Do you know anything about the nice things that are dumped into the trash," he asked me. I'm not sure why, but I can never remember lying to my dad. I would rather shoot myself, so the whole confession came forward. My dad tearfully absorbed the whole situation, then took me to a higher authority... God. We prayed. I have never ever been tempted to steal again. The example of my dad was the first influence toward the Savior who redeems.

As we read the New Testament, we can see the Person of Christ through the eyes of many witnesses who walked with Him and saw a sinless Man. We ask ourselves, when faced with life's difficulties, "What would Jesus do?" But there is a strong witness to the character of Jesus through the several personalities of the Old Testament as well. While they are not presented as sinless but faulty, the Bible faithfully points out the goodness in them. Together they create a strong picture of not only holy men of God, but ultimately of The Holy Man of God, Christ Jesus. These are to be seen as shadows or similitudes which look forward to Jesus Christ.

> *Now all these things happened unto them for examples: and they are written for our admonition, upon whom the ends of the world are come* (1 Cor 10:11).

Consider the following characters in the Bible:

Job:

God was so proud of Job, that he offered him as an example to Satan. He said to Satan, "Have you considered My servant Job? No one else on earth is like him, a man of perfect integrity, who fears God and turns away from evil." We know the story that follows as Satan was given permission to harass Job through loss of his wealth and family, followed by terrible boils. The Bible said that in all of this Job did not sin or blame God for anything. He asked, *"Should we accept only good from God and not adversity?"* Jesus prayed in the garden, *"If it be possible let this cup pass from me... yet, not My will but thine."* Although Job questioned why these things were happening to him, God rebuked him, and Job responded by covering his mouth (taking back his words). He said *"I had heard of you, but now my eyes have seen You."* Job, who was sinless in all of this, is a type of Jesus, who spoke not a word against His accusers. God not only restored Job's health, but doubled his wealth and blessed the last part of Job's life. Jesus, who was crucified, rose again to life eternal.

Noah:

God saw that man's wickedness was widespread on the earth and that every scheme of his mind was nothing but evil continually. God regretted that He had ever made man, and God was grieved in His heart. Then the Lord said, *"I will wipe off from the face of the earth mankind, whom I created, together with the animals, creatures that crawl, and birds of the sky – for I regret that I made them."* Noah, however, found grace (favor) in the eyes of the Lord. (Gen 6:5-8). Noah was a righteous man, blameless among his contemporaries; Noah walked with God. Though you and I are peculiar among our own contemporaries as followers of Jesus, our hearts are full of thanksgiving and praise having found grace in the eyes of the Lord through the cross of Jesus. We have accepted His offer to board the ark of safety and survive the sure judgement coming on an unbelieving world who has rejected Him. After the flood, Noah was given charge by God to *"be fruitful and multiply and fill the earth."* In like manner in worship of the Lamb who is worthy, we will in victory sing the new song: *"You made them a kingdom and priest to our God, and they will reign on the earth"* (Rev 5:10).

Abraham:

Your father Abraham was overjoyed that he would see My day; he saw it and rejoiced. The Jews replied, "You aren't 50 years old yet, and You've seen Abraham?" Jesus said to them, "I assure you: Before Abraham was, I am." At that they picked up stones to throw at Him (John 8:56-59).

- Abraham is called "a friend of God" (2 Chron 20:7; Isa 41:8; James 2:23). Why is he called a friend of God? Consider that God called him out of Mesopotamia (the land of Ur) and sent him to a land he did not know. He trusted that God knew what he was doing. *"Abraham believed God, and it was counted to him as righteousness"* (Gen 15:6; Rom 4:3; Gal 3:6). God planted his feet in Palestine and told him that land would be given to his descendants. He never saw the fulfilment of this promise, but according to Hebrews 11:10 *"he was looking forward to the city that has foundations, whose architect and builder is God."*

- God promised Abraham a son through Sarah. Sarah was well beyond child bearing years. When the miracle of pregnancy arrived by the message of an angel, Abraham laughed with joy.

- Later on, by faith Abraham obediently offered up Isaac, knowing what God had promised, namely that through Isaac God would bring forth a great nation and bless the whole earth.

- Sure enough, God presented a substitutionary ram caught in the thicket. *"God will provide."* What a statement of faith looking forward to the substitutionary atonement of the Cross of Jesus who knew no sin, but became sin for us.

- Though Abraham saw himself as a visitor in a land owned by others, his 175 years on this earth were spent taking God at His word.

- The Bible describes him as old and contented (Gen 25:8) even though he was buried in the cave of Machpelah near Mamre, in the field he had purchased from the Hittites. It reminds me of the borrowed tomb in which Jesus was buried (which was a fulfillment of prophecy). Although it is difficult to imagine Jesus being "contented" on the cross as He suffered, He was able to say *"It is finished."* There is no greater antecedent of a pronoun ever used. "It" is finished!

Isaac:[17]

The "offering up" of Isaac in sacrifice found in Gen 22:1-18 is to be compared with the passion and resurrection of Christ. Isaac was a type of Yeshua in that he was the only son of Abraham through whom would come the promise made to Abraham of blessing to the entire world; God sent His only begotten Son that our sin might be imputed to Him in the sacrifice of Calvary. The location of both sacrifices is significant because Isaac

was offered at Mariah, which 2000 years hence would be the Jerusalem where Jesus was crucified. Both sons carried the wood that was for their sacrifice and both were bound and placed on top of wood. Both sons were "resurrected" or "given back" to their fathers on the third day (compare Gen 22:4 with Matt 16:21). Both submitted willingly to their father. Both lives were given back to them: Isaac through the substitutionary ram and Jesus by His resurrection from the dead.

Joseph:

Joseph was the 11th son of Jacob, and he was aware through his God-given dreams that he would rule over his brothers. The young braggart made his brothers so angry with him that they would have killed him, but instead sold him providentially into slavery to some Midianite traders who took him to Egypt. The story spans from Genesis Chapters 37-50. Unlike his brothers Joseph not only avoided sinning against God but rose within the Egyptian hierarchy until he was "over all the land of Egypt," second only to Pharaoh. When Joseph's brothers came to Egypt due to the famine in their own land, they had to deal with Joseph whom they did not recognize. Joseph could have had them killed which is what they deserved. Instead, he revealed his identity to them, wept, and sent them home to get their father Jacob. To make a very long story very, very short, God worked this relationship with Egypt out such that Israel settled in the land of Egypt, in the region of Goshen. They acquired property and became fruitful and very numerous. After Jacob's death, Joseph's brothers still expected Joseph would repay them for their evil. They came to him bowing as his slaves.

Joseph wept, then told them not to be afraid. Then followed the kind words of Joseph to his brothers:

> *Don't be afraid. Am I in the place of God? You planned evil against me; God planned it for good to bring about the present result – the survival of many people* (Gen 50:19-21).

Joseph's kindness and forgiveness looks forward to the Christ who would pray, "Father forgive them." Jesus' crucifixion was meant for evil, but God used it for good.

Moses:

There can be little doubt that Moses is a picture of Jesus Christ. In the second giving of the Law, Moses prophesied: [18]

> *The Lord thy God will raise up unto thee a Prophet from the midst of thee, of thy brethren, like unto me; unto Him ye shall hearken* (Deut 18:15).

Jesus later would say, "If you had believed Moses, you would have believed Me" (John 5:46). The following comparison is remarkable:

1. Both were born at a time when Israel was under foreign domination (Moses-Egypt, Jesus-Rome).
2. Both had rulers that tried to kill them shortly after their births (Exod 1:15-22; Matt 2:16-18).
3. Both spent time in the wilderness before taking on their callings (Exod 3; Matt 4:1-11).
4. Both dealt with wicked kings (Pharaoh; Herod).

5. Both dealt with folks who hardened their hearts (Exod 8:15; Mark 6:45-52)
6. Both dealt with lepers (Num 12:10-15; Matt 8:1-4).
7. Both had the world offered them (Heb 11:24-27; Matt 4:8-9).
8. Both were shepherds (Exod 3:1; John 10:11).
9. Both fasted for 40 days (Exod 34:28; Luke 4:2).
10. Both climbed mountains (Exod 34; Matt 5:1).
11. Both were meek (Num 12:3; Matt 11:29; 21:5).
12. Both were envied (Psa 106:16; Matt 27:18).
13. Both did some writing (Exod 34:27; John 8:6-8).
14. Both have a connection to the law – Moses, humanly speaking, presented the law, but Jesus Christ fulfilled the law (Deut 31:9; Matt 5:17).
15. Both kept the Passover (Exod 12; Heb 11:28; Luke 22:11; Matt 26:17-10).
16. Both had connection to innocent blood (Deut 19:9-10; Deut 21:7-13; Matt 27:3-4).
17. Both sang (Exod 15:1; Matt 26:30).
18. Both had ministries to the nation of Israel (Exod 3:1-10; Matt 15:21-28).
19. Both did miraculous things (no references needed).
20. Both did miraculous things to or on large bodies of water (Exod 7:20; Exod 14:16,27; Matt 8:23-27; Mark 6:45-51).
21. Both fed hungry people in a wilderness (Exod 16; Mark 8:1-9).
22. Both provided water for thirsty people (Exod 15:22-25; John 4:10,14).
23. Both spoke of eternal fire (Lev 6:12-13; Matt 25:40-41).
24. Both spoke of future tribulation (Deut 4:30-31; Matt 24:21-22).
25. Both paid tribute (Num 31:41; Matt 17:24-27).
26. Both sent out 12 men (Num 31:41; Matt 17:24-27).

27. Both were called God's servants – "my servant" (Num 12:7; Matt 12:14-21).
28. Both were prophets (Deut 34:10; John 6:14). Note: If a prophet is one who speaks for God, Jesus, of course, could speak for Himself.
29. Both were priests (Exo 40; Heb 4:14).
30. Both were judges (Exod 18:13; John 5:24-30).
31. Both were teachers (Deut 4:5; John 18:20).
32. Both told wicked men to depart (Num 16:26; Matt 25:41).
33. Both met together on the Mount of Transfiguration (Matt 17:1-9).
34. Both are connected through the brazen serpent (Num 21:4-9; John 3:14).
35. Both had people weep when they died (Deut 34:8; John 20:11).
36. Both died but did not stay in their burial places (Deut 34:5-6; Jude 9: Matt 17;1-9; Matt 28).
37. Both were the subject of controversies concerning their dead bodies (Jude 9; Matt 28:11-15).
38. Both had important "dignitaries" interested in their dead bodies (Michael & the devil – Jude 9; the Pharisees, the Roman soldiers, and Pilate Matt 27:62-65; Mark 15:43-45).

Boaz:

The story of Ruth is one of blessing upon blessing. Ruth chose the God of Naomi, her mother-in-law, and in so doing chose salvation. Assuming that the reader is familiar with the story from the book of Ruth, consider the parallels between Boaz and Christ: [19]

| Boaz means "strength" | Jesus brings a strong grace to redeem |

Boaz was the kinsman.	Jesus was born of a woman.
Boaz was lord of the harvest.	Jesus was Lord of the harvest.
Boaz gave bread & wine to Ruth.	Jesus instituted the Lord's supper.
Boaz was the supplier of wants.	Jesus told us to ask anything and it shall be given.
Boaz was "kinsman-redeemer.	Christ, our brother, adopted us as sons and redeemed us by His blood.
Boaz bought Ruth for a price.	Paul referred to the ransom of the blood of Jesus when he said we "have been bought with a price."
Boaz was the bridegroom for Ruth.	Christ was seen as the Bridegroom of the church.

The Moabite Ruth was a foreigner in the land of her disinherited Hebrew mother-in-law Naomi. Included in the romantic aspect of the story, for Ruth is able to get the attention of Boaz, is a legal technicality from Leviticus 25:25, *"If one of your brethren becomes poor, and has sold some of his possession, and if his redeeming relative comes to redeem it, then he may redeem what his brother sold."*
Naomi knew that the unmarried and wealthy Boaz was her dead husband Elimelech's relative. Ruth, having won favor with Boaz, was able to inform him of Naomi who was in need of a kinsman-redeemer. Boaz was then able, according to the Law, to buy back

the land that was Elimelech's lifting Naomi and Ruth out of poverty.

Of course, Boaz married Ruth and we can see her named in the line of Jesus in Matthew 1:1. In this story the sin of Elimelech in leaving his own country during drought, rather than trusting the God
of Israel, led to his own death and that of his two sons leaving Naomi and Ruth without husbands or means. The return of Naomi and the choice of Ruth to stay with her mother-in-law leads to the

Christ-type in Boaz. Christ becomes our kinsman-redeemer by the cross of Calvary, by our belief in the salvation He brings and by His adoption of every believer as a son (Eph 1:5). In doing so He brings the more abundant life (John 10:10). Boaz represents the grace of God who brings blessing into every life who believes and trusts in Him.

Yet there is another wonderful insight in this story related to Ruth's request for Boaz to spread the corner of his garment over her since he was a kinsman-redeemer. In marriage the man brings his bride into his "tent" by covering her with his tallit (Ruth 3:9). The word 'tallit' is actually made up of two Hebrew words: TAL meaning "tent" and ITH meaning "little." Thus you have LITTLE TENT. Millions of Jews could not have fit into the tabernacle. Therefore, what was given was their own private sanctuary where they could meet with God... a prayer shawl. Its origin is given in Numbers 15:37-38 where God tells Moses to tell the people: *"Throughout the generations to come you are to make tassels on the corners of your garments, with a blue cord on each tassel.*" The blue threads are supposed to be reminders that they were God's people, blue symbolizing divine origin. But God had a better idea: "I will give you a new heart and put a new spirit within you; I will remove from you your heart of stone and give you a heart of flesh. And I will put my Spirit in you and move you to follow my decrees and be careful to keep my laws (Ezek 36:25-27). On the Day of Pentecost, Acts 2, the promised Holy Spirit was poured out. By invitation our bodies become the Temple of the Holy Spirit (1 Cor 6:19). We can live in the tent-of-meeting and talk to God anytime anywhere! This is our "tallit" given by grace through Jesus who said, "I will not leave you as orphans; I will come to you.... If anyone loves Me, he will keep my word, and my Father will love him, and we will come to him and make our home with him (John 14:18-23).

Samuel: [20]

There are such wonderful parallels between Samuel and Jesus that the typology is difficult to miss:

Samuel was born to a mother who had not conceived before. That she conceived was by the direct intervention of God. Through the Holy Spirit Mary conceived. Samuel was to be raised in Shiloh as a son to God. Jesus was the Son of God. Samuel was not raised by his real father but by Eli. Jesus was raised by Joseph who was not His father.

Samuel seemed to appear out of nowhere and he left no proper heirs to the office of the High Priest. He did not come out of the line of Aaron, nor did he leave a line of descendants to take his place. Our Lord seems to appear out of nowhere and He will leave no heirs to the office of High Priest, as He is a High Priest to God forever.

Samuel was dedicated to service at an early age as was Jesus. Samuel's parents were blessed at the Tent of Meeting for the choices that they had made with respect to Samuel. Joseph and Mary were blessed at the Temple when they brought Jesus (Simeon and Ana). As a youth, Scripture tells us that the boy Samuel was growing in stature and in favor both with Jehovah and with men (1 Sam 2:26). As a youth, Scripture tells us that the Child Jesus increased in wisdom and stature, and in favor with God and men (Luke 2:52).

The Psalm of Hannah dedicates Samuel to service to God while the song of Mary recognizes the fulfillment of God's promises to Israel. Both came to their ministry when the priesthood had become corrupted. Samuel essentially replaced the High Priest; no one during the time of Samuel or after his death are referred to as High Priests. Jesus Christ is the true High Priest. In His incarnation, He supplanted the existing priesthood. Samuel acted as an intermediary between God and man. Jesus is the ultimate intermediary between God and man.

David:

> *Even while Saul was king over us, you [David] were the one who led us out to battle and brought us back. The Lord also said to you, "You will shepherd My people Israel and be ruler over Israel."...Then David knew that the Lord had established him as king over Israel and had exalted his kingdom for the sake of His people Israel* (2 Sam 5:2, 12).

David was king by divine ordination. Christ was chosen from eternity to be the Monarch of mankind. This was predicted in Daniel 4:3, 34: *"His kingdom is an everlasting kingdom."* Jesus explained to Pilot, *"My kingdom is not of this world."* His is a kingship of divine origin and authority. Like the King of Kings David was chosen to *"shepherd My people Israel, and be ruler over Israel"* (2 Sam 5:2b). Jesus was both King and Shepherd. With the failure of Saul's reign, God anointed David, *"a man after God's own heart"* (1 Sam 13:14; Acts 13:22). Consider some of the attitudes in David that were perfected in Jesus. David loved the Word of God (Psa 119). Jesus' frequent quotation of Scripture reveals the same. In fact, Jesus is the Word of God (John 1:1). David loved to pray (Psa 116:1-2,12-13). Jesus would often rise early in the morning or slip away to pray privately (Luke 5:16). David loved to praise God as witnessed by the Psalms. He danced in joy before the Arc of the Covenant as it was returned. Jesus said, "To what shall I compare this generation? It is like children sitting in the market places, who call out to other children, and say "We played the flute for you, and you did not dance; we sang a dirge, and you did not mourn" (Matt 11:16-17). Jesus praised His Father publicly in prayer (Mat 11:25-26) as He did with His disciples in song (Matt 26:30). David practiced loyalty and unity (1 Sam 18:1; Psa 133:1) and knew the terrible pain of division within a family in his sons Amnon and Absalom. Jesus prayed earnestly that His disciples might be one (John 17:20-23) and brought peace and unity among those who would believe in his death on the cross (Eph 2:13-16), and yet He knew the betrayal of Judas Iscariot. David hated every false way (Psa 119:104). We know about Jesus' anger directed at the Temple money changers, and we read about his denunciation of the hypocritical Pharisees, scribes and lawyers (Mat 23:13-36).[21]

One cannot think about David without considering his beginnings as a shepherd for his father Jesse's flock. You can see a shepherd's heart, of course, in the Twenty-Third Psalm. You see it reflected in Isaiah: *"He will feed His flock like a shepherd; He will gather the lambs with His arm, and carry them in His bosom, and gently lead those who are with young"* (Isaiah 40:11), a lyric which appears so famously in the soprano aria of Handel's Messiah. Ezekiel in his prophecy continues the metaphor (Eze 34:23-31) which we will discuss in Part III. Jesus spoke of Himself as *"the good shepherd"* (John 10:11-18). David killed a lion and bear in protecting his sheep. Jesus said "the good shepherd gives his life for the sheep."

Daniel:

Daniel is that rare man in the Bible for whom is recorded no sin. If it were not for Romans 3:23 we would think him sinless. His devotion to prayer was like none other except Jesus of Nazareth. Someone has said that knowing the book of Daniel is the key to understanding all biblical prophecy, especially that which looks forward to the end times. Like Joseph in Egypt he was promoted to high rank in first the Babylonian and then the Persian Empire. One can speculate that he was greatly influenced by the reforms of King Josiah before Daniel was carried off with so many others to Babylonian captivity. His fidelity to the God of Israel seems almost Christ-like: *"The Son can do nothing of Himself, but what He sees the Father do; for whatever He does, the Son also does in like manner. For the Father loves the Son, and shows Him all things that He Himself does; and he will show Him greater works than these, that you may marvel"* (John 5:19b-20). We marvel at Daniel's God-given gift of dream interpretation. We notice that around Daniel good things happen, truths are learned and God is glorified. The uplifting message of Daniel would have lifted the weary hearts of the exiled Jews. Jesus lifted the hearts of a Roman occupied Israel. *"Come unto Me all ye who are weary and heavy laden and I will give you rest"* (Matt 11:28). *"My yoke is easy and My burden is light"* (Matt 11:30).

Esther:[22]

Until talking to Dr. Ronald Hunter I did not consider Esther. It is the only portion of the Bible that does not mention the name of God, yet is so important to understanding the sovereignty of God in His preservation of the Jews in Persia. The wicked Haman had concocted a scheme which would have caused the slaughter of all Jews in the 127 provinces under King Ahasuerus' rule. Her Uncle Mordechai's message to Esther was the rhetorical question: "Who knows whether you have not come to the kingdom for such a time as this?" (Esther 4:14) Esther called for a fast among her people, and the frightened Israelites complied. To make a long story short through the Jewish Queen Esther, her people were spared and Haman was hung.

Here is the picture: Esther stands as a bookend to Moses in the salvation of Israel. Moses led them out of slavery in Egypt, and Esther made possible their survival in Persia. But the nation of Israel in both instances is under the judgment of God because of its idolatry. In the Exodus we see the worship of the Golden Calf even as their leader is receiving the Ten Commandments from God. In Persia we can reflect on the withdrawal of God from the temple because of their idolatry and their refusal to listen to the prophets God sent to warn them. Finally, there was no remedy and God used Assyria, Babylon and Persia in their expulsion from the Promised Land, the destruction of Jerusalem and the temple. With their deliverance from Egypt the Passover is celebrated on the 15th of the first month of Nissan. The deliverance from Haman in Persia is celebrated on the 15th of the last month of Adar and is called Purim. At the request of Esther to fast, the people afflicted themselves through the sacrifice of food and drink for three days. Christ sacrificed Himself for us on the cross of Calvary and in three days he arose from His grave. In the Jews instance they were delivered from Haman's scheme after the three days of fasting. Esther put on royalty to approach the king. Christ was glorified to ascend to the throne in heaven. Esther's intercession to deliver her people was granted. Christ's intercession to deliver His people was granted.

Jonah

I have included Jonah here, not because he was Christ-like in character, but because of the unmistakable symbolism of three days in the belly of the great fish, after which God brought him up from the deep and a sure death to proclaim salvation to the people of Nineveh. Unlike Jesus Jonah was reticent to pray "Yet not my will but Thine be done." Instead he tried to flee from God's difficult assignment. We know the story: God sent a storm which surely would have destroyed the ship on which he sailed. Miserable and depressed in having run from God, Jonah instructed those with whom he sailed to throw him overboard that they at least might be spared. But God prepared a great fish which swallowed him up. Then, Jonah prayed his version of "not my will but Thine be done" as he gulped what oxygen he could from the belly of the great fish for three days and three nights. "I called to the Lord in my distress, and He answered me.... I will fulfill what I have vowed" (Jonah 2:2,9). Then God commanded the fish, and it vomited Jonah onto dry land. Like Jesus he spent three days in the realm of the dead then was raised to new life. From there in obedience he preached in Nineveh with such success that they proclaimed a fast and dressed in sackcloth, from the greatest to the least. Jonah proclaimed that God was about to destroy them, they believed Jonah, and repented! As a result, God relented and spared them. Of course, Jonah was angry and complained that God had caused him to take part in this act of mercy toward Israel's enemy. "I knew that You are a merciful and compassionate God, slow to become angry, rich in faithful love, and One who relents from sending disaster" (Jonah 4:4). As God had compassion on the heathen of Nineveh, so He loved the whole world in sending His Son to die on the cross for all of us.

Hosea:

We know Hosea not only because of His denunciation of sin in Israel, but because of the assurance given that God's love would win out in the end. Hosea becomes a Christ-type with his willingness to take back his adulterous wife, Gomer. After reading Hosea, it's only natural to think of Jesus, the sinless Son of God, coming to a sin-prone planet. He demonstrated His love and commitment and yet was rejected and betrayed. Matthew applied Hosea 11:1 to the infant Jesus exiled in Egypt with His parents: *"When Israel was a child, I loved him, and out of Egypt I called My son."* But by far the most compelling portrait of Jesus is Hosea's marriage to Gomer, a woman who would be unfaithful to him. The picture is of our God who loves us even as we stray away from Him and into sin. As Hosea bought back his wife despite her adultery, so God, through His Son Jesus, identified with our plight and lovingly paid the cost of our freedom with His blood.[23]

PART II – CHRIST IN FORM: THAT WE MAY SEE

Introduction

Michael Angelo's depiction of God on the ceiling of the Sistine Chapel in Rome.

I am reminded of the very handsome "Anglo-Saxon Jesus" painting that hung on the back wall of our sanctuary. It always bothered me simply because Jesus skin tone was more likely Mediterranean. However, we have little idea what he looked like other than *"He had no form or comeliness, no beauty, that we should desire Him"* (Isa 53:2). As far as the Sistine Chapel ceiling goes, the Bible tells us simply that no one has seen God the Father (John 1:18). Adam heard God walking in the garden and hid from Him. He also heard his voice. But nowhere does it say that He saw Him. What do we make of Genesis 1:26, *"Let us make man in our own image"*? God is a spirit, and it may very well be that the essential part of man that is eternal is also a spirit. It may be that *"Our own image"* is a reference to godly character traits, creative talents and even *"the mind of Christ"* (1 Cor 2:16). The New Testament says that when we are with Him, we will be like Him, for we shall see Him as He is (1 John 3:2). We need to be careful that we do not play god in our attempts to make Him in man's own image. This would be a god we might think we can live with, but does he bare any resemblance to the God the Bible?

Furthermore, we see the biblical revelation of Christ presented in a historical fashion with progressive clarity and without contradiction. The atheist view of Christianity, and religion in general, is thought to be evolutionary. First, someone had a hallucination. Next, the place where the supposed god appeared was hallowed. Then, many more legendary accretions accumulated in oral fashion. Finally, some of these stories were written down by unknown individuals. Still later, other unknown men, called redactors, edited the original stories – the end product being a sacred text for that religion.[24] While this may sound like the Koran or the Book of Mormon, it certainly does not sound like the Bible of Christianity. The entire Bible stands or falls as one unit. If certain parts or elements were legendary or untrustworthy, it would be impossible to tell where the myth ends and the truth begins. The evangelical believer accepts the Bible for what it claims to be – the infallible, inerrant, verbally inspired account of God's dealings with mankind. It is to be interpreted according to its plain grammatical and historical sense. The appearances in the Old Testament of the pre-incarnate Son of God took place at definite historical moments and were accorded to historical personages. None are taken as apparitions, but as actual events experienced through their five senses while men and women were fully awake. The Bible presents the Christophanies as actual occurrences in the history of mankind. They should be accepted as such.

In Jonathan Swift's satire, *Gulliver's Travels*, he visits several lands, each ones citizens uniquely different from the other. In Lilliput the people are tiny and think that the giant Gulliver's watch must be his god, because he always refers to it before he does anything. In the land of Brobdingnag, the citizens are giants compared to Gulliver and they conceive of Gulliver at first as a dangerous vermin, then a curiosity. In successive travels he discovers the flying island of Laputa, which rules over the land of Balnibarbi below by throwing rocks at rebellious citizens from above. From the port of Maldonada he takes a short side-trip to the island of Glubbdubdrib which brings historical perspective as he discusses the "ancients versus moderns." From there he travels to Luggnagg where he encounters struldbrugs, who suffer the infirmities of old age but are unfortunately immortal. While in Japan, he performs the ceremony of "trampling on the crucifix," and his final voyage takes him to the country of the Houyhnhnms, a race of noble talking horses, who rule over a race of human beings in their deformed and savage state, called Yahoos. Gulliver wishes to remain among the Houyhnhnms but, alas, is a Yahoo himself and is rejected. Much to his chagrin he must return home to live with his fellow Yahoos (in case you wondered where that slang expression came from). With each race of creatures from Lilliput to the land of the Houyhnhnms Gulliver can see that the conceptions of each are dependent upon their own points of view.

Thus the Houyhnhnms conceive of their god as a horse.

I suspect that Swift may have intended Houyhnhnm to represent the unpronounceable JHWH.

This satire colorfully makes a point for us regarding self-serving idolatry. The Israelites in despicable syncretism mixed Baal worship in with their shallow view of Jehovah. Without God's Word we are left to our own deceptions regarding God. Were it not for the revelation of Scripture we would be lost in the fiction we create out of our own fears, needs and imaginations. This leaves us confused, insecure and without the possibility for redemption.

The Bible as God's revelation of Himself to mankind presents God in type, form and prophecy in the Old Testament so that its readers will understand and receive the Christ of the New Testament. This section will treat the appearances of God the Son in the Old Testament in what Dr. John F. Walvoord attempts to distinguish as "formal theophany"[25] - that is, God appearing in human form. Therefore I have titled this section "Christ in Form: That We May See."

Moses was not allowed to see God's face, for God said "no man shall see Me and live." God hid Moses in the cleft of the rock and "covered him with His hand while His glory passed by revealing His "hinder-most parts" (Exod 33:21-22). Yet there is a part of God that we are allowed to see. That is the incarnate Son of God who walked among us. Let us now consider the pre-incarnate Son of God as revealed in the Old Testament.

CHAPTER 8
CHRISTOPHANY

We have shown that Christ is revealed in "type" throughout the Old Testament. It was many years before I realized that Christ had also revealed Himself in "form" in the Old Testament, because these occurrences are referred to as the appearance of "The Angel of the Lord." But they are very different from the other appearances of angels. For one thing this Angel is worshiped. The worship of angels is forbidden. One reason angels are rendered invisible to human sight may be that, if they were seen, they would be worshiped (Rev 19:10; 22:9). Man, who is so prone to idolatry as to worship the works of his own hands, would hardly be able to resist the worship of angels were they before his eyes.[26] As great and impressive as the mighty angels are, the writer of Hebrews compares them to a superior Jesus Christ (Heb 1:4-14). The church at Colossae (Col 2:17-19) had been invaded by false teachers who were teaching a false humility and the worship of angels as a part of the means to spirituality. It seems these teachers were claiming special mystical insights by way of visions in connection with their worship of angels. For this they were strongly repudiated by the Apostle Paul. Although the mighty created angels are sent out to serve those who are going to inherit salvation, they are not to be worshiped and cannot compare to the eternal uncreated Son of God. We, along with the angels, worship Jesus Christ.

Blessing and honor and glory and dominion to the One seated on the throne, and to the Lamb, forever and ever! (Rev 5:13)

However, the Angel of Jahweh is properly worshiped as we shall see. That is the strongest indicator in answering the question, "Who is the Angel of the LORD?"

Christophany is by definition an Old Testament appearance of Christ, the second person of the Trinity. Most theophanies (Old Testament appearances of God) are, in fact, Christophanies. Of the 214 usages of the Hebrew term for "angel," about one-third of them refer to "the Angel of the LORD." Dr. John Walvoord makes the following assessment of these Old Testament appearances. "It is safe to assume that every visible manifestation of God in bodily form in the Old Testament is to be identified with the Lord Jesus Christ."[27]

Why was it necessary for God to appear in Christophany? Is it that they would not have believed had He not? I don't think so. More often than not it was the voice of God or the word of the Lord which came to Old Testament characters. For example when Elijah escaped the murderous Jezebel, he despaired for his life. He thought himself to be the last remaining hope, and God taught him a lesson. He could not see or hear God in the wind, the earthquake or the fire, but instead heard God in a still small voice. The word of the Lord came to Elijah and assured him that He had a thousand in Israel that could speak for Him who had not yet involved themselves with idolatry. One message that is derived from this episode is that God is not limited to prophets like Elijah to speak for Him. He does not rely on theophanies or christophanies or thunderous sound, but can speak even in a still small voice (1 Kings

19:13). So we need to understand that He chose from time to time to speak to men in terms that they could both see and hear. One would think it an advantage for a man to both see and hear from a live visible speaker. Yet, how He chooses to appear to a person, whether it is to encourage, warn, administer justice or minister compassion, is entirely up to God. Here we intend to discuss those instances where God appeared in human form. These appearances were temporary and to certain individuals.

There are several such appearances of this kind in the Old Testament that are very different from the other many visitations of angels. In these instances the angel is called "The Angel of Jehovah," usually translated "The Angel of the Lord." At first I just figured, well, they are all angels of the Lord. But this usage is to be distinguished from "an angel of the Lord," or "God's ministering angel" and any other of the phrases pertaining to named or unnamed angels. He appears singularly in several instances. Because the precise identity of "The Angel of the Lord" is not given in the Bible, we must decide who this figure is. The evidence toward the identity of this messenger of JHWH is quite strong. Let's consider the following:

1. He appeared to Hagar, the mother of Ishmael by a spring of water in the wilderness (Gen 16:7-13). "You are the God who sees me," she observed; "I have now seen the One who sees me." He later called to Hagar from heaven (Gen 21:17-20).

2. He appeared to Abraham at the oaks of Mamre (Gen 18:1-33).

3. The Bible simply says that the Lord appeared unto Isaac (Gen 26:2, 24). Although the form is not described, it could

not be God the Father who no man has seen. By implication this is the Second Person of the Trinity.

4. He spoke to Jacob in a dream (Gen 31:11-13).

5. He appeared standing next to Jacob in the dream of Jacob, wrestled with Jacob and then spoke to him as the Lord (Gen 32:24-32). Also see Genesis 35:1, 9-13 where God appeared to Jacob.
6. The Angel of the Lord is referred to by Jacob as Redeemer (Gen 48:15-16).

7. He appeared to Moses from the burning bush. Throughout the dialogue at that burning bush it was also declared that He was no less than Yahweh who spoke at that time causing Moses to hide his face from him (Exod 3:2-14; Acts 7:29-39).

8. He stood in Balaam's path, confronting him with a drawn sword (Num 22:22-35)

9. He appeared to Joshua as "Commander of the Lord's Army" (Josh 5:13-6:5).

10. He appeared in Bochim to the people of Israel to scold them for not listening to God. He told them that He would not deliver them from the Canaanites and that their gods would be a trap for them (Judges 2:1-4).

11. Later, the Angel of the Lord came and called Gideon to deliver Israel from the power of Midian (Judges 6:1-23).

12. He appeared to Manoah and his wife, the mother of Samson. When Manoah asked for the "Angel of the LORD" to also appear to him, He reappeared to Manoah as He had appeared to his wife. After conversation with him, He ascended in the flame of the altar implying the sacrifice was in worship of the Lord Himself. (Judges 13:3-23).

13. Moreover, the Angel of the Lord is regarded as a "Redeemer," who saves Israel from evil (Isa 63:9)

14. Nebuchadnezzar apparently saw a protective Christ in the fiery furnace with Shadrach, Meshach and Abed-Nego. He said, *"Look! I see four men loose, walking in the midst of the fire; and they are not hurt, and the form of the fourth is like the Son of God."* Dan 3:24-26

15. Here Zechariah the prophet sees and overhears the Angel of the Lord in conversation with God" (Zech 1:8-17; 2:1-5).

16. He is seen rebuking Satan and is later spoken of by Zechariah as "like God." (Zech 3:1-2; 12:8)

Several things make these instances of "The Angel of the LORD" stand out: [28]

- "The Angel of the Lord" is distinct from Yahweh, yet identical with Yahweh. The presence of the Angel of the Lord is the same as the presence of the Lord, Himself. He accepts worship due only to God. If He were only an ordinary angel, regardless of His stature, he would have refused the act of worship and corrected the behavior as happens elsewhere in Scripture.

- The Angel of the Lord speaks as God, identifies Himself with God, and claims the prerogatives of God.

- The Angel of the Lord definitely identifies Himself with Yahweh. "I will multiply your descendants," He tells Hagar. The Angel of the Lord is God Himself.

- Gideon built an altar to The Angel of the Lord and worshipped. You do not worship angels.

- The doctrine of the trinity is in play here, because The Angel of the Lord is equal with God, yet distinct from Yahweh.

- Godly men and women of the Bible recognized this angel as God. He is referred to as Yahweh.

The key in translation is the definite article, "the," in "The Angel of the Lord." Whenever it appears, there are unique differences in the experience involved. There are several choices here:

1. The Angel of the Lord is like any other angel, and he is speaking for the Lord.
2. The Angel of the Lord has special credentials to accompany God.
3. The Angel of the Lord is the pre-incarnate Christ.

Historically, the apostles and those who followed in the second century, though mentioning Christ's preexistence, Clement of Rome, Polycarp, Ignatius and others, seldom mentioned the Christophanies. The apologists in succeeding centuries, such as

Justin Martyr and Theophilus of Antioch, were in general agreement that the Angel of the Lord was the preincarnate Christ. However, the Nicene and Post-Nicene church fathers claimed that Christ was not totally equal with God the Father, thinking him a created being, "His only-begotten son". Augustine maintained that the theophanies in human form were the functions of angels who represented God. That opinion held for more than a millennium. The Protestant theologians of the sixteenth and seventeenth centuries held the position of the early church that the Messenger was deity, Christ Himself appearing in human form. Thus, for the most part the Reformation brought back into view the doctrine of the Christophanies that prevailed among the apologists of the second century. For the most part this view holds true for the vast majority of Bible-believing fundamentalists and other conservative, evangelical Christians today.[29]

The evidence seems to support overwhelmingly the view that – the Angel of the Lord was Christ the pre-incarnate Son of God, appearing on earth during the time of the Old Testament.[30] His appearances are called theophanies, appearances of God, or more accurately Christophanies, appearances of Christ.[31] Jesus the Son of God is most certainly not an angel. All angels are creatures; He is the Creator, superior to any of the angels (Heb 1:4).[32] It seems likely that the title "Angel" stood for His office, not His nature. Christ in this form was sent as a messenger and indeed is used in this general sense throughout scripture (e.g. Rev 3-4). Thus, it is quite evident from His being spoken of as God, bearing the name of Jehovah, speaking as God, possessing divine attributes and receiving worship, that this "Angel" who appeared in the Christophanies, while exercising the office of a messenger, was indeed none other than the
Diety Himself.[33]

James Borland summarizes:[34]

1) The Bible frequently speaks of the Angel of the Lord as being God.
2) It is important that He bore the name of "Jehovah," viz. The Angel of Jehovah.
3) He spoke as God, e.g. "I am the God of thy Father..." (Exod 3:6). The final, and in some ways the highest, revelation is that embodied in the words of the Messenger of Jehovah in Genesis 22:11-12, 15-18. Here the great Abrahamic covenant is reaffirmed and even enlarged, in the strongest of terms, and according to biblical Writ Abraham never again meets God.
4) He had divine attributes, prerogatives and authority including His creative, causative power, the power to give life (e.g. Gen 16:10 and Exod 3:20). Only God forgives sin (Exod 23:21), or has the power of life over death (Gen 22:12).
5) He received worship and was honored with sacrifice (e.g. Judges 13:19)

The man-like form of the Christophany being properly emphasized, let it also be reaffirmed here that human form is not equivalent to full participation in human nature with body, soul and spirit. This was reserved solely for the unique and permanent incarnation of Christ.

And the Word became flesh, and dwelt among us, and we saw His glory, glory as of the only begotten from the Father, full of grace and truth (John 1:14).

He is the image of the invisible God, the firstborn[35] of all creation (Col 1:15).

...who, being in the form of God, did not consider it robbery to be equal with God, but made Himself of no reputation, taking the form of a bondservant, and coming in the likeness of men. And being found in appearance as a man, He humbled Himself and became obedient to the point of death, even the death of the cross (Phil 2:6-8).

What was from the beginning, what we have heard, what we have seen with our eyes, what we have looked at and touched with our hands, concerning the Word of Life – and the life was manifested, and we have seen and testify and proclaim to you the eternal life, which was with the Father and was manifested to us (1 John 1-2).

We understand that in Christ in the New Testament was the fulfillment or completion of God's revelation of Himself. Yet, it is clear that in the Old Testament God sent His Son, sometimes in human form called Christophany, in order to bring fellowship, encouragement, direction and physical sustenance. At other times He was sent to warn or to announce judgment, to issue promises or to confirm covenants. Finally, He called others into service; He commissioned them for a particular mission. In general, the Bible does not dwell in detail on the form of the Christophany, although indicating the form of a man. It seems more important to see the purpose or message, which reminds us that the Second Person of the Trinity is the Word of God (John 1:1-2). The Christophanies were not mini-incarnations. They did not partake of our humanity but rather simulated its likeness, even as the Holy Spirit appeared "in a bodily shape like a dove" at Christ's baptism (Luke 3:22). The Christophanies anticipated the incarnation only as a type pictures in some ways the later reality. There is a similarity in form, not an identity in nature.[36]

It is our position that the human-form theophanies were the exclusive function of God the Son. The similarities of the two ministries, as well as the purposes of the Christophanies, argue for this view. There is a divine division of labor among the persons of the triune God, and the human-form theophanies are in line with all that is known of the Son's activities. It seems quite appropriate that such theophanies be termed Christophanies.[37]

Finally, there are several ways in which the writers of the New Testament refer the deeds of the Messenger of Jehovah to none other than Christ. In Hebrews 12:18-26, the shaking of Mount Sinai is clearly attributed to Christ, while the Old Testament refers it to Jehovah. 1 Corinthians 10:4 says that Christ was the supplying source on the Exodus and in the wilderness. Hebrews 11:26 plainly says Moses bore "the reproach of Christ," while the Pentateuch states he acted at the behest of the Angel. Luke 1:15-17 portrays John the Baptist as going before Christ, in fulfillment of Malachi's prediction about the "Messenger of the covenant," who is equated with the Angel of the Lord. John 12:38-41 asserts what when Isaiah beheld Jehovah, even though in a vision (Isaiah 6), he saw Christ.

PART III – CHRIST IN PROPHESY: THAT WE MAY BELIEVE

Introduction

We have laid the ground work for Part III by showing that Christ appears in the Old Testament both in type and form. This adds strength to the short survey put forward in this section of Messianic prophecy. There is no stronger indicator than the words of Jesus Himself when He said in John 5:39, *"You [Jewish people] diligently study the Scriptures (which at the time were the 39 books of the Tanak/Old Testament].... These are the Scriptures that testify about Me."* We would have liked to be there as an investigative reporter when Jesus rebuked Cleopas and another disciple as they walked along the road to Emmaus on that first Easter Sunday.[38]

> *"How foolish you are, and how slow of heart to believe all that the prophets have spoken! Did not Christ have to suffer these things and then enter His glory? And beginning with Moses and all the prophets, He explained to them what was said in all the Scriptures concerning Himself"* (Luke 24:25-27).

What might have been the specific passages that Jesus explained to them? These are the passages that detail the coming of the Messiah. It is ironic and pathetic at the same time that so few recognized Him when there were so many Messianic prophecies with ``such overwhelming detail. Luke records two people who did know that Jesus was the Messiah. Simeon was described as "waiting for the Consolation of Israel." Here is a devout Jew who was impacted by the words of Isaiah, *"Comfort ye, comfort ye my people, saith your God. Speak ye comfortably to Jerusalem, and cry unto her, that her warfare is accomplished, that her iniquity is pardoned.... And the glory of the Lord shall be revealed, and all flesh shall see it together: for the mouth of the Lord hath spoken it"* (Isa 40:1-2a, 5). The Bible says that the Holy Spirit was on Simeon and that it had been revealed to him by the Holy Spirit that he would not see death before he had seen the Lord's Christ, so he came to the temple at exactly the time that Joseph and Mary brought the child Jesus to the Temple for the normal presentation of a first-born son to God. Simeon took the child up in his arms, blessed God, then said this: *"Lord, now You are letting Your servant depart in peace, according to Your word; for my eyes have seen Your salvation which You have prepared before the face of all peoples, a light to bring revelation to the Gentiles, and the glory of Your people Israel"* (Luke 2:29-32). This was immediately followed by the recognition of the eighty-four year old Anna, a prophetess described as resident within the temple "serving the Lord with fastings and prayers night and day." The Bible says she came just at that instant and gave thanks to the Lord. What's more, she spoke of Him to all those who looked for redemption in Jerusalem. Unlike Simeon and Ana the scribes and Pharisees are neither described as just and devout, nor as waiting for the consolation of Israel, nor as serving God with fastings and prayers night and day. Jesus was pretty hard on them: *"Woe to you, scribes and Pharisees, hypocrites! For you shut up the kingdom of heaven against men; for you neither go in yourselves, nor do you allow those who are entering to go in"* (Matt 23:13). He had cried out to the Jews *"He who believes in Me, believes not in Me but in Him who sent Me. And he who sees Me sees Him who sent Me. I have come as a light into the world, that whoever believes in Me should not abide in darkness. But if that person rejects Me, and does not receive My words, the very words I speak will judge him in the last day* (John 12:44-50).

As we read the Old Testament it becomes clear that the people of Israel are not a super-race but are, rather, chosen. They are chosen to bring redemption to the human race through a "seed." But, "seed" is ambiguous in Hebrew: it can refer to the descendants or it can refer to an individual descendant. As the revelation unfolds, we can see that it is the latter, for the promise surely points to a second Adam, a Seed who is appointed like Seth, called like Noah, chosen like Shem, and made a blessing to all the earth as the Seed of Abraham.[39]

"*Who has believed our report? And to whom has the arm of the Lord been revealed?*" So begins the prophecy regarding Christ in Isaiah 53. Jesus stood up and read from Isaiah 61 when he entered the synagogue in Nazareth on the Sabbath day. After reading this Messianic prophecy, he sat down and said "*Today this Scripture is fulfilled in your hearing*" (Luke 4:21). Only by reading the prophecies regarding Christ can we know that they have been fulfilled and will continue to be fulfilled with His Second Coming. In his book, *The Messiah in the Old Testament*, Walter Kaiser was able to identify 65 direct predictions of Jesus' comings in the Old Testament. Taken as a whole, the real presence of Jesus as the Angel of the Lord, direct personal messianic foretellings and any or all types of real and typological prophecies of Jesus' first or second coming, theologians have found from 348 to 574 verses depending on how they are classified.[40] Let's consider some of these Messianic prophecies.

CHAPTER 9
MESSIANIC PROPHECY IN THE PENTETEUCH

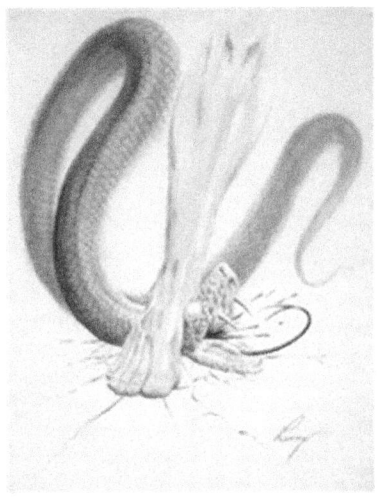

ADAM

In God's condemnation of the serpent in Genesis is found the first proclamation of the promise of God's plan for the whole world in the Edenic prediction:

And I will put enmity between you and the woman, and between your seed and her Seed; He shall bruise your head, and you shall bruise His heel (Gen 3:15).

Verse 13-14 name the serpent as the tempter of Eve in God's curse. A good starting place in understanding this text is to identify this tempter. It is not so much that the serpent walked upright and must now crawl on his belly. *"On your belly you shall go"* and *"you shall eat dust"* are figures of speech vividly picturing a defeated foe.[41]

In his temptation of Eve we note his intelligence, perception, speech and knowledge. He knows more than Adam and Eve. He speaks as if he has access to the mind of God. The serpent of the temptation is the serpent of the final conflict; he is someone whom a future male descendant of the woman will strike with a crushing blow to his skull.

And the dragon stood before the woman who was ready to give birth, to devour her Child as soon as it was born. She bore a male Child who was to rule all nations with a rod of iron. And her child was caught up to God and His throne (Rev 12:4b-5).

And the dragon was enraged with the woman, and he went to make war with the rest of her offspring, who keep the commandments of God and have the testimony of Jesus Christ (Rev 12:17).

So the great dragon was cast out, that serpent of old, called the Devil and Satan, who deceives the whole world; he was cast to the earth, and his angels were cast out with him (Rev 12:9-10).

The devil, who deceived them, was cast into the lake of fire and brimstone where the beast and the false prophet are. And they will be tormented day and night forever and ever (Rev 20:10).

Who then is the "seed" or "offspring" mentioned in this text? Clearly the term "seed" is a generic term for the entire race that came from the woman on the one hand, while the "seed" of the serpent embraces all the evil race derived from him. However, the noun "seed" may include the one who represents the whole group as well. This fact opens this text up to its Messianic possibilities.[42]

NOAH

After the flood, Noah became a farmer and planted a vineyard. Having imbibed more of his product than he should have one night, he was drunk and naked in his tent and presumably passed out or asleep. The story is that Ham, the younger son, saw the nakedness of his father and told his two brothers, Shem and Japheth, about it outside the tent. It may be that seeing his father's nakedness was not Ham's chief offense. The following verses imply that Ham made fun of his father, and that this news reached Noah after he awoke. The older boys Shem and Japheth took a garment, hung it over their shoulders and backed in to cover their father's nakedness. Their faces were turned away and they honored their father in this manner. When Noah awoke from his bender, he knew somehow what his younger son had done to him and pronounced a curse on Canaan which named him a servant to his brothers, especially Shem.

Blessed be the Lord, the God of Shem, and may Canaan be his servant. May God enlarge Japheth, and may he dwell in the tents of Shem; and may Canaan be his servant (Gen 9:26-27).

Shem is apparently the central figure of this prophecy. The question is this: Who is the referent of the pronoun "he" in "may he dwell"? I will not detail the rationale behind the best answer to that question but refer the reader to the expertise of Dr. Kaiser. The meaning of Genesis 9:27 is God's announcement that His advent will take place among the Shemites, later known through the Greek form of their name as the Semites (Jews).[43] Taken with the Genesis prophecy we can see clearly that God promises to come in His advent in the line of a woman (Gen 3:15), the human side of the messianic redemption, and as God on high to dwell among the people of Shem (Gen 9:27), the divine side of the coming Messiah. These two lines of Messianic prophecy, the human and the divine, henceforth develop side by side in Scripture.

ABRAHAM

From among the Semitic tribes to whom God had given His promise to dwell among them, He called one Semitic couple, Abram and Sarai, to leave the plush surroundings of Ur in southern Mesopotamia and go about 1100 miles away to an unnamed land He would show them. This "call of Abram" begins a new era in history and a new epoch in the disclosures about the promise-plan of God with its central character, the Messiah.

On at least six occasions the divine promise was announced to Abraham (Gen 12:1-3,7; 13:14-18; 15:4-5,13-18; 17:1-8; 18:17-19; 22:15-18). On two other occasions the same prophetic words were given to Isaac (26:4, 23-24), and twice more this same covenant, with its same promises, was repeated to his son Jacob (28:14-15; 35:9-12). God made eight promises to Abraham in Genesis 12:1-3:[44]

1. He would make him into a great nation;
2. He would bless him;
3. He would make his name great;
4. Abraham and his seed would be a blessing to others;
5. God would bless those who bless him;
6. He would curse those who cursed Him;
7. Through Abraham and his "seed" God would be the channel of blessing to all the peoples on earth; and
8. God would give to Abraham's "seed" the land he had entered after leaving Ur of the Chaldeans.

Abraham and the descendants ("seed") of Shem were to be the medium through which all the world would be blessed. The word "seed" must be understood in some exclusive way, for not all of Abraham's biological progeny are intended (e.g. none of Keturah's children or the child Hagar bore Abraham). There is a narrowing of the promise likewise in the posterity of Isaac (Esau is excluded) and of Jacob (where the blessing bypassed the eldest brothers but was given to the fourth son, Judah).

JACOB AND JUDAH

Jacob's family increased to 12 sons from which are derived the 12 tribes of Israel. This amounted to some 70 people including grandchildren and dependents by the time the family left for Egypt (Exod 1:5). But it was Jacob's fourth son, Judah, whom God singled out to be the channel through which the messianic line would continue. Jacob's blessing, like Noah's, serves as a prophecy:

Judah, your brothers shall praise you; your hand shall be on the neck of your enemies; your father's sons shall bow down to you. Judah is a lion's whelp; from the prey, my son, you have gone up. He couches, he lies down as a lion, and as a lion, who dares rouse him up? The scepter shall not depart from Judah, nor the ruler's staff from between his feet, Until Shiloh comes, and to him shall be the obedience of the peoples. He ties his foal to the vine, and his donkey's colt to the choice vine; He washes his garments in wine, and his robes in the blood of grapes. "His eyes are dull from wine, and his teeth white from milk" (Gen 49:8-12).

The interpretation of this prophecy depends in large measure on the meaning of the word "Shiloh." It should be translated "until it comes to whom it rightfully belongs."[45] Two things are foretold in this verse: the tribe of Judah will not cease to exist as a people, and Judah will have a government of its own until the Messiah appears on the scene. Shiloh is best understood as a cryptic form of a personal name for the Messiah. The world will one day come in homage and submission to Shiloh, that is, to the One to "whom [dominion rightfully] belongs."

That at the name of Jesus every knee should bow, of those in heaven, and of those on earth, and of those under the earth, and that every tongue should confess that Jesus Christ is Lord, to the glory of God the Father. (Phil 2:10-11).

The blessing Jacob gave in this situation looked forward to what God would do. As Joseph had served, so must Israel serve, but in God's own time the blessing to the nations must come through the seed of Abraham. The ruler of God's choosing would eventually come, and the scepter would be His. The ancient prophecy is recalled again in the last book of the Bible. John weeps because there is no one who can open the book of God's decrees. One of the elders in the heavenly throne room responds, "Do not weep! See, the Lion of the tribe of Judah, the Root of David, has triumphed. He is able to open the scroll and its seven seals" (Rev 5:5).[46]

BALAAM

For this prophesy we need to re-visit the Christophany mentioned in Chapter 4, that of Balaam the prophet in Numbers 22:22-35. The scene is in the fortieth year of the Exodus wandering in the desert, as they approached the land of the Moabites. Frightened by this mass of humanity, the king of Moab, Balak, sought to hire the prophet Balaam to place a curse on the Israelites. At first Balaam refused because Yahweh had forbidden him to go, stating that a blessed people could not be cursed. But since Balak was persistent, Balaam capitulated even though it displeased the Lord. Three times when situated to throw a spell or curse on Israel, Balaam ended up blessing Israel instead.

A Star shall come out of Jacob; a Scepter shall rise out of Israel (Num 24:17).

Under the inspiration of God, Balaam prophesied a powerful ruler who would rise from Israel to gain victory over its enemies. A "star" and a scepter" who would arise from Israel in days to come (Num 24:14). The picture painted by Balaam of the "star," "scepter," and "ruler," the man who would arise out of Israel and be awesome in his conquests and decisive in his actions, is a picture of the coming Messiah. Indeed, "Who can live when God does this?" This portion mainly depicts what will take place at the second advent of Messiah. He will literally clean house of all evil and all opposition to His rule and reign.47

MOSES

The LORD your God will raise up for you a Prophet like me from your midst, from your brethren. Him you shall hear, according to all you desired of the LORD your God in Horeb in the day of the assembly, saying, "Let me not hear again the voice of

the LORD *my God, nor let me see this great fire anymore, lest I die." And the* LORD *said to me: "What they have spoken is good. I will raise up for them a Prophet like you from among their brethren, and will put My words in His mouth, and He shall speak to them all that I command Him"* (Deut 18:15-18).

In Chapter six we have already discussed the life of Moses as a type of Christ. So it should not surprise anybody that this messianic prophecy would compare Him to Moses. The coming prophet would be[48]

1. An Israelite (Deut 18:15,18)
2. "Like" Moses (Deut 18:15,18)
3. Authorized to declare God's word with authority (Deut 18:18-19)

He would perform miracles in public before the nations, as Moses had done (Deut 34:11-12), not in private. He would be a lawgiver as Moses had been and a mediator who would pray earnestly for the people as Moses had done (Exod 32:11ff., 31-35). He would also be a deliverer, just as Moses had been used by God to deliver his people from slavery in Egypt. When the people in Jesus' time saw the miracle of the feeding of the five thousand, they exclaimed, *"Surely this is the Prophet who is to come into the world"* (John 6:14). And, they said the same thing when they heard Him teach at the Feast of Tabernacles (John 7:40). Philip found Nathaniel and announced to him, *"We have found the one Moses wrote about in the Law, and about whom the prophets also wrote"* (John 1:45). Even the Samaritan woman concluded that Jesus must be that "prophet" (John 4:19,29) who was to come. The connection was also made in Peter's second sermon (Acts 3:11-26) as well as

Stephen's sermon (Acts 7:37). Jesus confirmed the messianic nature of Deuteronomy 18 when he addressed the scribes and Pharisees:

> *You search the Scriptures, for in them you think you have eternal life; and these are they which testify of Me. But you are not willing to come to Me that you may have life.... If you believed Moses, you would believe Me; for he wrote about Me. But if you do not believe his writings, how will you believe My words?* (John 5:39-40, 46)

JOB

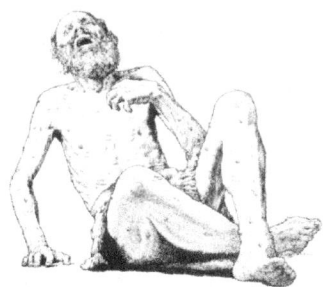

If the book of Job is to be placed in the period of the patriarchs (c.2100-1800), as we believe he is to be placed, [49] then there are four texts in Job that should be added to the six in the Pentateuch. [50]

In Job 9:33 he is responding to Bildad's first speech where Job is desperately longing for "a Mediator" who could represent him before God. Only someone who can go between both God and a human could affect the needed reconciliation. One can see the logic building for some person who will be no less than the Son of God in order to bridge the gulf. Jesus Christ has made peace with everything in heaven and on earth by means of His blood. Through His Son God has reconciled all things to himself (Col 1:20). The apostle Paul put it to the Corinthians this way: God has "reconciled us to Himself through Jesus Christ... that is ...not imputing [our] trespasses to [us]" (2 Cor 5:18-19).

In Job 16:19-21 he makes his appeal to "a Witness in heaven" who will act as his advocate. John tells us "we have an Advocate with the Father, Jesus Christ the righteous" (1 John 2:1b).

In Job 19:23-27 he makes a number of definite assertions about the coming Messiah. Job sees that there is "a Redeemer." *"I know that my Redeemer lives and that he shall stand at last on the earth; and after my skin is destroyed, this I know, that in my flesh I shall see God."*

In Job 33:23-28 once again we see Job long for a mediator, a messenger who will act as "an Interpreter." Job envisions the messianic Person as exceeding by a thousand-fold the ordinary angels (v.23), and as One who will redeem him from the pit (v.28). Without a doubt Job presents several poignant anticipations of the Messiah.

CHAPTER 10
MESSIANIC PROPHECY LEADING UP TO DAVID

Even though Moses and then Joshua prepared the people well for crossing over into the Promised Land between the Jordan River and the Mediterranean Sea, though God kept his promise to Abraham and Moses that He would give Israel a land, though God kept His promise to Joshua:

Be strong and courageous, for you shall cause this people to inherit the land that I swore to their fathers to give them... Do not be frightened, and do not be dismayed, for the Lord your God is with you wherever you go (Josh 1:6, 9b),

...though the Lord gave to Israel all the land that He swore to give to their fathers, though they took possession of it and settled in it, though not one of their enemies had withstood them, though not one word of all the good promises that the Lord had made to the house of Israel had failed, the period following Joshua's death until the appearance of Samuel is best characterized by a cycle of Israel falling into idolatry, being enslaved by their enemies, Israel crying out to the Lord for deliverance, God raising up a judge, Israel being delivered, Israel serving the Lord and then falling again into idolatry. In chapter two of the book of Judges is the story of Rahab's faith who harbored the Jewish spies and, like Ruth after her, chose the God of Israel and found herself in the lineage of Jesus (see Matt 1:5). Toward the end of the period of the Judges (1375-1050 B.C.) we find another remarkable woman:

HANNAH and God's "Anointed One"

Here is the story of a frustrated woman who prayed to God to remove the stigma of her inability to have children. Hearing her pray so earnestly and silently Eli the priest at first thought her drunk. She made a vow that if God would give her a son, she would give him to the Lord. Eventually God did give her the son named Samuel, one of the most important figures in the history of God's promise-plan of redemption. She kept her vow and took Samuel to the tabernacle to be raised by and minister along-side the high priest, Eli. Samuel would play a key role in moving from the age of the judges to that of the king. Little did Hannah realize that her son would be the prophet whose actions prepared the way for David through whom the promised Messiah would come. Her prayer-song of praise to God who answered her prayer (1 Sam 2:1-10), is messianic in part (verses 9-10). Here the "king" is introduced. This follows with the promise that God will also "exalt the horn of his anointed," and that He "will judge the ends of the earth." Similar terminology comes in Psalms 2 and 110 which will be considered ahead. It is certain that Hannah's words are messianic, for this is confirmed by Peter in the New Testament (Acts 3:24): *"All the prophets from Samuel on... foretold these days,"* i.e. the coming of the Messiah. Samuel makes no reference to any messianic prediction except in Hannah's prophecy, which Samuel records. The "anointed One" in this text is clearly the coming Messiah.[51]

ELI and "the faithful Priest"

By way of background to Eli, we note that God ordained Aaron, the brother of Moses, and his family to officiate as priests before him (Exod 29:9). As Israel came to the end of their wilderness pilgrimage, God made a covenant with Aaron's grandson Phinehas for an "everlasting priesthood" (Num 25:12-13). Aaron and his family could hardly be called "everlasting." Eli had been a dismal failure as a father, raising two wayward sons who were wicked. Furthermore, Eli, himself, failed to honor God in the manner he carried out the duties of his office as priest. Though *"the word of the Lord was rare in those days and there was no frequent vision"* (1 Sam 4:1b), there came an unnamed *"man of God"* who prophesied before Eli (1 Sam 2:27-36). Referring to a time yet to come the prophesy given was that *"Then I will raise up for Myself a faithful priest who shall do according to what is in My heart and in My mind. I will build him a sure house, and he shall walk before My anointed forever"* (1 Sam 2:35). Only Jesus always did what pleased the Father (John 8:29). Only the Messiah would also be a faithful priest over God's house (Heb 3:6).

NATHAN and the Eternal Kingdom of David

God had promised Abraham that kings would someday come from him (Gen 7:6,16). He repeated this promise to Moses. In Samuel's day the people could not wait for God's timing, so they tried to get the judge Gideon to become king. Gideon declined the offer, asserting the principle, "The Lord will rule over you" (Judges 8:23). Abimelech was made king for a short time and that ended in tragedy both for Abimelech and his "kingdom." As a result of their impatience, God allowed Samuel to anoint Saul as king. But he did not prove to be God's choice. He was looking for a man *"after God's own heart."* That sounds entirely like the prophecy above: I will raise up for Myself a man who will *"do according to what is in My heart and in My mind."* He became Yahweh's king who would rule Israel for the next forty years. Nathan's prophecy to David is third in importance to Gen 3:15 ("He shall crush his head") and Gen 12:2-3 (the promise to Abraham).[52]

Now the word from the unnamed prophet becomes clear: Instead of having David build a "house" for the Almighty, God will make a "house" out of David (2 Sam 7:13). After the word of the Lord came to Nathan informing him that David would not build the temple that he so desired to build, but instead, his son would build, God gave David this confidence through Nathan's prophecy:

> *"When your days are fulfilled and you rest with your fathers, I will set up your seed after you, who will come from your body, and I will establish his kingdom. He shall build a house for My name, and I will establish the throne of his kingdom forever. I will be His Father and He shall be My son"* (2 Sam 7:12-14a).

I'm sure that David was disappointed that God would not allow him to build a temple and move the Arc of the Covenant into it. But, he responded in prayer to the Lord, *"Who am I, O Lord God? And what is my house...?"* He continued, *"Now, O Lord God, the word which You have spoken concerning his house, establish it forever and do as You have said."* And further, he prayed, *"Now therefore, let it please You to bless the house of Your servant, that it may continue before you forever; for You, O Lord God, have spoken it, and with Your blessing let the house of Your servant be blessed forever"* (2 Sam 7:18-29).

In his prayer five times David uses the phrase "O Lord God" (or Adonai Yahweh). It is used nowhere else in Samuel or Chronicles. But it is used when God promised a "seed" to Abraham (Gen 15:2,8). David sees this prophecy as nothing less than a "charter for humanity," an everlasting reign. Jacob had seen that the leadership of the tribes would fall to his fourth son, Judah; Balaam had predicted that a star and a scepter would arise out of Jacob that would crush all his enemies. But Nathan now predicts that the one family in Judah on whom the mantle of ruling will descend is David's family, And that rule, kingdom, and authority will not be limited; three times he emphasizes that it will be "forever" (2 Sam 7:16). This is repeated with the same emphasis in Psalm 89:

> *I will establish his offspring forever and his throne as the days of the heavens... His offspring shall endure forever, his throne as long as the sun before me. Like the moon it shall be established forever, a faithful witness in the skies* (Psa 89:29,36-37.

That is why the angel Gabriel announces to Mary, the mother of the Messiah, that "the Lord God will give Jesus the throne of his father David, and he will reign over the house of Jacob forever and that His kingdom will never end (Luke 1:34-33). Psalm 89 is titled "A Maskil of Ethan the Ezrahite." Inspired by God to write this psalm, Ethan expands on the prophecy of Nathan: "*I will be His Father and He shall be My son,*" to say:

> *He will call out to me, "You are my Father, my God, the Rock my Savior." I will also appoint to him my firstborn, the most exalted of the kings of the earth* (Psa 89:26-27).

David has come to an understanding that this all depends only on God and not one whit on David. Nathan's prophecy, then, predicts several important new features about the coming Messiah:[53]

1. The Messiah will come from David's flesh and seed;
2. He will be David's heir;
3. He will also be God's natural son;
4. He will have a kingdom, rule, and reign that will never end; and
5. He will surely come one day in the future.

Thus we move from the "seed of the woman," who will be victorious over Satan, to the "seed of Abraham," who will be a blessing to all the earth, to the "seed of David," who will have a rule that will never end. From here we will discuss messianic references in the Psalms and then some 39 predictions of the Messiah in the Old Testament prophets.

CHAPTER 11
DAVID AND THE PSALMS

J. Barton Payne has counted 101 verses of direct prophecies of Messiah occurring in thirteen different psalms.[54] Most of the messianic psalms belong to the Davidic period. One is by Solomon, one without attribution and another by one of the sons of Korah. We give our attention here to nine psalms:

THE REJECTION OF MESSIAH (Psalm 118)

No author or title line is given for this psalm, and were it not for verse 22, we probably would not consider it messianic. The oft quoted first and twenty-fourth verses draw us into this song of thanksgiving for His everlasting love:

Oh, give thanks to the Lord, for He is good! For His steadfast love endures forever! This is the day that the Lord has made; let us rejoice and be glad in it.

In praise and worship the psalmist joyfully sings *"Open to me the gates of righteousness... this is the gate of the Lord,"* an immediate reference to the gates of the Temple. Continuing on the theme of Temple architecture the psalmist now mentions the cornerstone in verses 22-23:

> *The stone that the builders rejected has become the cornerstone. This was the Lord's doing; It is marvelous in our eyes.*

Of course, the cornerstone is very important in the construction of a building. Solomon's Temple was 30 cubits high (about 51 feet). If the cornerstone were off by a tiny fraction of an inch, they could have been erecting a leaning tower! From the cornerstone the entire building is plumbed and measured. Modern architects have discovered what must have been the cornerstone of Zerubbabel's (Herod's) temple. It is 3 ft. 8 in. high by 14 ft. long, and it rests on solid rock to a depth of 79 ft. 3 in. below the surface. On the selection of the cornerstone rests the success of the entire structure. It must be selected with patience and exactitude. Apparently the stone of Psalm 118:22 had at first been rejected, laid aside, then re-discovered as the ideal cornerstone. Isaiah mentioned this in his messianic prophecy:

> *Behold, I lay in Zion a stone for a foundation, a tried stone, a precious cornerstone, a sure foundation; Whoever believes will not act hastily* (Isa 28:16).

Jesus used the allusion in His quotation of Psalm 118:22-23 (Matt 21:42). Peter in his second sermon clarified the metaphor:

> This Jesus is the stone that was rejected by you, the builders, which has become the cornerstone. And there is salvation in no one else, for there is no other name under heaven given among men by which we must be saved (Acts 4:11-12).

I remember a gospel folk song taught me by my father:

> O where is the Stone that was hewn out of the mountain;
> O where is the stone that came rolling through Babylon;
> O where is the stone that was hewn out of the mountain,
> And came down through the kingdoms of the world.

Of course, "that came rolling through Babylon" is a reference to Daniel's messianic vision from captivity. Finding a Bible (The Word, Jesus Christ) my dad would raise it over his head and sing:

> This is the Stone that was hewn out of the mountain;
> This is the Stone that came rolling through Babylon;
> This is the Stone that was hewn out of the mountain,
> And came down through the kingdoms of the world.

In a similar way, David, the father of the promised heir and coming Messiah, was also rejected. His father, Jesse, did not consider him suitable material for anointing as king (1 Sam 16:11). His brothers scorned him and misunderstood him (17:28-20). Saul had tried on numerous occasions to kill him while his first wife, Michal, daughter of Saul, despised him (2 Sam 6:20-23). Only Judah accepted David as king at first, for the northern ten tribes preferred to follow Saul's house, despite all that Saul had tried to do to David (2 Sam 1-3). But what human beings had rejected, God designed to make the foundation of what he had planned to do from the beginning: David was chosen to be king over the whole nation.⁵⁵

THE BETRAYAL OF MESSIAH (Psalms 69 & 109)

The messianic aspect of psalms 69 and 109 can be found in the fact that all the enemies of David, his throne, his dynasty, and his kingdom, are finally epitomized in one final hostile adversary upon whom God's judgment must fall. Is it any surprise that Judas became that opponent of Messiah? Does not John 13:27 record that Satan entered into Judas as he conceived the plot to betray Jesus, just as Psalm 109:6 declares? And was not the place of Judas taken over by Mathias after he committed his treachery and ended up hanging himself (Acts 1:16-20)?⁵⁶

While Psalm 69, a psalm of David, certainly portrays David's suffering, verses five and six seem to preclude this suffering from being messianic: "O God, you know my folly; the wrongs I have done are not hidden from you." However George Frideric Handel for his oratorio, The Messiah, chooses verse 20 as recitative for the tenor area, "Comfort Ye:"

> *Thy rebuke hath broken His heart: He is full of heaviness. He looked for some to have pity on Him, but there was no man, neither found He any to comfort Him (Psa 69:20).*

Handel took license in his translation, because the psalm is expressed in the first person, while Handel places it in the third person: "my heart" becomes "His heart," etc. King David, the human Davidic officeholder, has been hated and accused without cause or reason (verses 5-6). In Jesus day the religious leaders hated the fact that His healing and preaching drew such crowds. It appeared to them to be dangerous insurrection if not a threat to their own tenuous authority over the people. The theme arises in the New Testament with Jesus most strongly at his mock trials. They could not produce two witnesses against him except by false accusation. Since His works were all good, th ey could only accuse Him of healing on the Sabbath and of blasphemy due to His claim to be the Son of God. But, that would not have flown in a Roman court if their desire were his execution. So, they made something up. They accused him of sedition, plotting against Caesar. He claimed to be "King of the Jews," they asserted before Agrippa. That was a convenient lie. Even though Pilot found Him guiltless, he allowed the crowd to decide the sentence of crucifixion.

> *They also gave me gall for my food, and for my thirst they gave me vinegar to drink* (Psa 89:21).

> *They gave Him sour wine mingled with gall to drink* (Matt 27:34).

Here it seems to be a deliberate messianic reference. The next can be related to Judas Iscariot, the betrayer of Jesus:

> *Let their dwelling place be desolate; let no one live in their tents. For they persecute the ones You have struck, and talk of the grief of those You have wounded. Add iniquity to their iniquity, and let them not come into Your righteousness. Let them be blotted out of the book of the living* (Psa 89:25-28).

> *See! Your house is left to you desolate; for I say to you, you shall see Me no more till you say, "Blessed is He who comes in the name of the Lord!"* (Matt 23:38-39; Luke 13:35)

And with regard to Judas specifically:

> "The Son of Man goes just as it is written of Him, but woe to that man by whom the Son of Man is betrayed! It would have been good for that man if he had not been born." Then Judas, who was betraying Him, answered and said, "Rabbi, is it I?" He said to him, "You have said it." (Matt 26:24-25).

Jesus knew the heart of Judas, and He knew the prophecy:

> *Even my own familiar friend in whom I trusted, who ate my bread, has lifted up his heel against me* (Psa 41:9).

Like Saul, who committed suicide when he realized his case was hopeless, Judas went away and hanged himself (Matt 27:1-10). It would have been better had he never been born.

Psalm 109:6-19 may have even stronger messianic reference to Jesus and to His betrayer. Ten judgments are introduced against one specific adversary:

1. The enemy will have Satan at his right hand (v.6).
2. He will be found guilty when tried (v.7a).
3. His prayers will be regarded as sin (v.7b).
4. The one opposing God's anointed will die prematurely (v.8a).
5. This betrayer's office will be filled by another person (v.8b).
6. His children will be orphaned and his wife widowed (v.9).
7. His creditors will seize everything the enemy has worked for (v.11).
8. No one will show compassion on the opponent's descendants (v.12).
9. The betrayer's sons will die childless (v.13).

10. The guilt of his sin and the iniquity of his family will be remembered against them (vss.14-15).

David, of course did not know the name of Judas, but his role, demeanor, motivating forces and resulting judgments are all clearly marked. This act of betrayal, Peter argues under inspiration of the Holy Spirit, was spoken "long ago through the mouth of David concerning Judas" (Acts 1:16).

THE DEATH AND RESURRECTION OF MESSIAH (Psalms 22 & 16)

The most dramatic and convincing predictions the psalmists made occur here. The sufferings detailed here are amazing: the piercing of the hands and feet, the body stretched upon the cross, the intense thirst and the division of the garments. David, himself, did experience suffering, but under a revelation from God he witnesses suffering of one of his offspring, presumably the last in that promised line, that far transcends anything that came his way.

The Psalm begins with Jesus' own cry from the cross, *"Eli, Eli, lama sabachthani"* (which means "My God, my God, why have you forsaken me?" (Psa 22:1; Matt 27:46). It was here that Jesus experienced for the first time His worst anguish. When He became sin for us, there had to be complete separation from God that He had never known before. David's words became His at that moment.

One can parallel the tone of the messianic prophecies of Isaiah as Psalm 22 progresses: "I am a worm" (Psa 22:6; Isa 41:14); [I am] not a man, scorned by men" (Psa 22:6; Isa 53:3); [I am] despised by the people (Psa 22:6; Isa 49:7). The mocking continues: "He trusts in the Lord; let the Lord rescue him. Let him deliver him, since he delights in him." Curiously, that is the precise speech that was hurled at Jesus on the cross (Matt 27:39-43). As the Psalm continues, twice he mentions his "mother" (not his father!) as the one bringing forth this descendant in the line of David. The description continues: "He feels exhausted, poured out like water, his bones are out of joint, his heart has turned to wax and melts away, his thirst is raging, he is near to dying, his hands and feet are pierced, his skin has become so taut that his bones stick out. In verse 18 he watches helplessly as they gamble for his garments (Matt 27:35).

In verses 22-31 the tone changes to triumph as *"all the ends of the earth"* are to remember what has been done for them and must turn to the Lord. Dominion belongs to the Lord and He rules the nations. Thus, the death and sufferings of this One who came in David's line and who suffered far more than David ever did is the means by which God will usher in his universal rule and reign over everything. In fact, every kingdom of the world will be given to Him; nothing will be left outside of His domain, even those who have *"gone down to the dust shall bow before Him"* (vs. 29).

> *Therefore God also has highly exalted Him and given Him the name which is above every name, that at the name of Jesus every knee should bow, of those in heaven, and of those on earth, and of those under the earth* (Phil 2:9-10).

If one can attach Psa 22:31 ("He has done this" with Jesus last words on the cross ("It is finished"), this surely indicates that the psalm was on His mind and comforted Him.

Peter quoted Psalm 16 in his Pentecost address in Acts 2:27, commenting that David foresaw and spoke about the resurrection of Christ when he sang the words of Psalm 16:10. The apostle Paul likewise uses this passage in his message at Antioch (Acts 13:35).

For You will not leave my soul in Sheol, nor will You allow Your Holy One to see corruption (Psa 16:10).

THE CONQUERING KING AND ENTHRONED MESSIAH
(Psalms 110 & 2)

The best overall statement of the Messiah in the Psalms can be found in Psalm 110 and Psalm 2. First, with Psalm 110:1 & 4, there are two divine utterances: "Sit at my right hand until I make your enemies a footstool for your feet;" and, "You are a priest forever, in the order of Melchizedek." Priest and King, both statements are directed toward Yahweh whom David calls, "my Lord." Messiah is indicated as the Father invites the Son of God to sit alongside Himself. The scepter given to Him in verse 2 is reminiscent of the promise made to Judah in Genesis 49:10, that the scepter would not depart from Judah until it was given to the one to whom it belonged. That scepter, with the authority it symbolized, now appears in Psalm 110. The Messiah will carry out the judgment against the nations to such an extent that the earth will be heaped with the dead corpses. In God's judgment blood will flow from "the winepress" as high as a horse's bridle (Rev. 14:20).

Psalm 2 begins with the question, *"Why do the nations rage so furiously and the peoples imagine a vain thing? The kings of the earth rise up, and the rulers take counsel together against the Lord, and against His anointed" (vs.1-2)*. I first became familiar with this passage from Handel's base air in the 1741 *Messiah* oratorio. The tenor recitative continues "He that dwelleth in heaven shall laugh them to scorn; the Lord shall have them in derision" (vs.4), immediately followed by the tenor air *"Thou shalt break them with a rod of iron; thou shalt dash them in pieces like a potter's vessel"* (vs.9). All resistance against

Yahweh and His Anointed One will be fruitless. Handel sees the implications of this total victory and immediately follows with the famous chorus based on Revelation 19:6 *"Hallelujah! For the Lord God Omnipotent reigneth."*

MESSIAH AS TRIUMPHANT KING (Psalms 68 & 72)

Psalm 68:18-19 is the grand messianic verse of the psalm:

> *You have ascended on high, You have led captivity captive; You have received gifts among men, even from the rebellious, that the Lord God might dwell there. Blessed be the Lord, Who daily loads us with benefits, the God of our salvation! Selah*

You have ascended on high is an allusion to the ascension of Jesus Christ (Mark 16:19; Acts 1:9) where He sits at the right hand of God. Paul in his Ephesians Chapter 4 explanation of gifts given according to the measure of Christ's gift fully quotes Psalm 68:18 (Eph 4:8). The ultimate goal of Messiah's advent, ascension, and endowing His people with gifts is that all may enter into His final victory over the rebellious – increasingly as the ages move on and finally in that last day, when the grandest of all victories is consummated in Christ's second coming.

Psalm 72 attributed to Solomon is written in the future tense; not even Solomon in all his glory could have fulfilled what is said here. Psalm 72 represents the Messiah as ruling in righteousness, justice and peace as he receives the homage of the nations of the world. While verse 2, *"He will judge Your people with righteousness, and Your poor with justice,"* could apply to Solomon, it lines up with other messianic texts regarding the Righteous Judge (Isa 9:7; 11:2-5; 32:1). Messiah's reign will be like fresh rain falling on earth (v.6) is a messianic figure of speech that occurs elsewhere (e.g. Hos 10:12; Joel 2:23).

> *His name shall endure forever; His name shall continue as long as the sun. And men shall be blessed in Him; all nations shall call Him blessed (Psa 72:17).*

The name of Messiah will endure forever, because all the nations of the earth will be blessed in Him. This prayer is clearly based on the Abrahamic promise of Genesis 12:3; 22:18; and 26:4. This is the single promise-plan still in effect in David and Solomon's day. Ever since God announced it, almost one millennium before to the patriarchs, it has not changed in its basic thrust. Its focus and center is on the Anointed One, the Messiah, who will come in the line of Abraham, Isaac, Jacob, Judah and David; but its benefits are to be made available to all the families of the earth. The psalmist closes with a doxology (vss. 18-19) recognizable in the Isaac Watts hymn:

> *Jesus shall reign where'er the sun,*
> *Does its successive journeys run.*
> *His kingdom spread from shore to shore,*
> *Till moons shall wax and wane no more.*

CHAPTER 12
NINTH & EIGHTH CENTURY PROPHETS

The promise of the Messiah as a blessing to the entire world was not only a prediction for what God was going to do in the future, but it was also a doctrine by which men and women lived in their contemporary situations. In fact, in the time of David and the prophets, it was as much a present reality as a forecast for the future.

This messianic doctrine preached by the prophets, sung in the Psalms, built into the temple, rising with the smoke of every sacrifice, the great quickener of Israel's conscience, the bulwark against idolatry, the protection of patriotism from despair, the comfort under affliction, the warning against temptation, the recall to the wandering; in short, a doctrine of salvation offered to Israel and every Israelite; more than this, Israel's missionary call to the nations, inviting all without exception to turn to the service of Yahweh – is the doctrine of the promise of blessing, made to Abraham and Israel, renewed in David and his seed, to be eternally without recall, and including the human race in its scope.[57]

Although the promise-plan of blessing to the world varies in its different stages through which revelation passes, it is uniform in its essential character throughout the Old Testament.[58]

THE MESSIAH AS TEACHER OF RIGHTEOUSNESS (JOEL 2:23)

Be glad then, you children of Zion, and rejoice in the Lord your God; for He has given you the former rain faithfully, and He will cause the rain to come down for you – the former rain, and the latter rain in the first month (Joel 2:23).

Dr. Walter C. Kaiser Jr. makes a strong case that the Hebrew 'moreh' should be translated "teacher" instead of "rain."[59]

And ye sons of Zion, joy and rejoice, in Jehovah your God, for He hath given to you the Teacher for righteousness, and causeth to come down to you a shower, sprinkling and gathered – in the beginning (YLT).

Normally the word 'hammoreh' in Hebrew means "the teacher," and the phrase "hammoreh litsdaqah" is similar to the expression "teacher of righteousness."[60] Dr. Kaiser in choosing "the teacher of righteousness" over "new rain" as the proper rendition of "hammoreh litsdaqah" shows that this "teacher" must be the Messiah for several reasons:

1. The Hebrew text uses the definite article with "teacher;" Joel has a distinct person in mind.

2. The term 'moreh' which appears in the singular eight times in the Bible, is rendered "teacher" in all cases and is translated that way in several ancient versions: the Vulgate, the Targum, and the Greek translation of Symmachus.

3. What clinches the identity of the Messiah as a teacher is the connection of the word "righteousness" with the preposition "to" or "for". God the Father will give to the people of Zion a teacher who is the personification of righteousness. (See, for example, Isaiah 52:11).

4. This term "righteousness cannot be applied as a quality of "rain," for it is an ethical and moral term.

5. That same connection between rain and righteousness is seen in Psalm 72:5-7, for the Messiah is the One who gives life and produces the abundance of grain and fruit. And His coming will also be linked (speaking of rain) with a mighty downpour of the Holy Spirit in the distant future.

So it seems that Joel deliberately plays on the word 'moreh' meaning "teacher" and "rain" to indicate that the coming of God's Teacher will signal, as one mark, the coming of the autumn and spring rains in their season. God will send a "downpour" of His Holy Spirit on his people in "those days" (2:29).[61]

And it shall come to pass afterward that I will pour out My spirit on all flesh; your sons and your daughters shall prophesy, your old men shall dream dreams, your young men shall see visions. And also on My menservants and on My maidservants I will pour out My Spirit in those days (Joel 2:28-29 NKJV).

Both these prophecies in Joel are confirmed in the New Testament. Peter quotes Joel 2:28-32 in his sermon at Pentecost (Acts 2:17-18). Peter's quotation of Joel was to correct a perception that those coming from the upper room were drunk. These signs were that the Holy Spirit had come in a mighty way! Jesus had told them to wait until they were endued with power from on high. Then they would be His witnesses, first in Jerusalem. Jesus had explained that He must go away for the Promised Holy Spirit to come. When the Holy Spirit comes, *"He will testify of Me. And you also will bear witness, because you have been with Me from the beginning"* (John 15:26-27). He went on to say that the Holy Spirit, the Spirit of truth, would guide them into all truth; *"for He will not speak on His own authority, but whatever He hears he will speak; and He will tell you things to come. He will glorify Me, for He will take of what is Mine and declare it to you. All things that the Father has are Mine. Therefore I said that He will take of Mine and declare it to you"* (John 15:13-15). This is the "righteous Teacher" of Joel; this is the Representative of Jesus Christ which is still at work in the life of every believer.

THE MESSIAH AS THE SECOND DAVID (HOSEA 3:4-5)

The story of Hosea and Gomer, already mentioned in Chapter 1, exemplifies the love of God toward Israel:

> *Then the Lord said to me, "Go again, love a woman who is loved by a lover and is committing adultery, just like the love of the Lord for the children of Israel, who look to other gods and love the raisin cakes of the pagans. So I bought her for myself for fifteen shekels of silver, and one and one-half homers of barley. And I said to her, "You shall stay with me many days; you shall not play the harlot, nor shall you have a man – so, too, will I be toward you." For the children of Israel shall abide many days without king or prince, without sacrifice or sacred pillar, without ephod or teraphim. Afterward the children of Israel shall return and seek the Lord their God and David their king. They shall fear the Lord and his goodness in the latter days* (Hosea 3:1-5).

The life of Hosea moves from object lesson to prophecy regarding Christ with these words. Just as Hosea cannot overlook his wife's time of sowing wild oats, God cannot overlook the nation's apostasy and idolatry. The disobedient nation of Israel will live for many days without the advantage or security of a king, prince, sacrifices, or even the idolatrous forms of worship. That has been the case from the days that the northern kingdom was carried off in captivity in 722 B.C. by the Assyrians up to today. Hosea also seems to have anticipated an increasingly secular state since the Babylonian exile, for it will not even have a stomach for idols in her new religion-less state of being, much less for God and the ritual connected with His worship (not withstanding the short revival of Ezra and Nehemiah following the return from captivity). To this day Israel is a secular state. But God will remember His covenant with Eve, Shem, Abraham, Isaac, Jacob and David "in the last days" – a phrase repeatedly used to point to the eschatological time when Messiah arrives as King over all. Kaiser points out five aspects of the promise of Messiah which are made here:[62]

1. The Messiah will return when Israel returns to their Lord.

2. The Messiah will be a descendant of David, for he is called "David their king" (vs.5). That is, of course, that he is the culmination of the Davidic line.

3. He will be a great king who will rule over those who fear Him.

4. The northern house of Israel that broke away from Judah after the days of Solomon will render allegiance to someone in the line of David, only He will be far greater than David

ever was. Most preeminently, the Messiah is closely identified with Yahweh, yet at the same time distinguished from Him.

5. Afterward the children of Israel shall return to the Lord

"Afterward the children of Israel shall return and seek the Lord their God and David their king. They shall fear the Lord and his goodness in the latter days" (Hos 3:5).

This can only mean Messiah "in the latter days," His second advent.

THE MESSIAH AS THE RAISED HOUSE OF DAVID (AMOS 9:11-15)

*"On that day I will raise up the tabernacle of David, which has fallen down, and repair its damages; I will raise up its ruins, and rebuild it as in the days of old; that they may possess the remnant of Edom, and all the Gentiles who are called by My name," Says the L*ORD *who does this thing. "Behold, the days are coming," says the L*ORD*, "When the plowman shall overtake the reaper, and the treader of grapes him who sows seed; the mountains shall drip with sweet wine, and all the hills shall flow with it. I will bring back the captives of My people Israel; they shall build the waste cities and inhabit them; they shall plant vineyards and drink wine from them; they shall also make gardens and eat fruit from them. I will plant them in their land, and no longer shall they be*

pulled up from the land I have given them," says the LORD *your God* (Amos 9:11-15).

The literal meaning of the Hebrew in verse 11 (tabernacle which has fallen down) is "hut" or "booth." The "rebuilding" uses the golden age of David as its contrasting reference. When one looks at the modern state of Israel, one sees an amazing economy, flourishing agriculture, the discovery of oil, a very successful high-tech industry and the return of more and more Jews worldwide to Israel. Theirs is a country which is multi- national, including many Arabs, who are free to vote and thrive in a parliamentary democracy comparable to Great Britain. All of this may be seen as a partial fulfillment of the prophecy. The "plowman has most certainly overtaken the "reaper." Even in what should be a tenuous existence surrounded by its enemies Israel has the assurance that God has "planted them in their land and that no longer shall they be pulled up from the land God has given them." It should interest the student of prophecy that the flag of Israel is centered with the shield of David, the hexagram. God is raising up the "tabernacle of David." As the ministry of tourism explains, "The Menorah has been brought back from its long exile, thus symbolizing the end of the Diaspora."

THE MESSIAH AS THE BREAKER (MICAH 2:12-13)

> *"I will surely assemble all of you O Jacob, I will surely gather the remnant of Israel; I will put them together like sheep of the fold, like a flock in the midst of their pasture; they shall make a loud noise because of so many people. The one who breaks open will come up before them; they will break out, pass through the gate, and go out by it; their king will pass before them with the Lord at their head."*

Of the world's 14.2 million Jews, over 6 million, about 43%, reside in Israel. Over 5 million reside in the United States. About 3 million are dispersed throughout the world. Will there be something one day to draw the other 8 million to Israel? Will the United States suffer some circumstance that incentivizes its 5 million to return to Zion? These are questions we can't answer, but Micah pictures those not in the Promised Land as sheep in a pen waiting to be released to go out to pasture (vs.12). Micah speaks of "one who breaks open the way" out of the pen for his sheep. Some translations render this the "Breaker." The prophecies speak frequently about the re-gathering the nation of Israel. While there have been several "re-gatherings" beginning with the return from Babylon under Zerubbabel in 536 B.C., none of these seem to be what the prophet is referring to.

This flock is waiting for a leader, who will free His penned-up sheep. Thus the grand messianic aspect of this text is unveiled. Three titles are given to this leader:

1. BREAKER: He is the "Breaker," the "One who breaks open the way"(vs.13). Micah may be thinking of the Good Shepherd or he may be seeing the Messiah who smashes through ranks of the besieging army that has surrounded the remnant of Israel. In that case, we have a picture of a conqueror – the Messiah, who will come and rescue His people.

2. KING: This Breaker was also known as "their King." The royal theme of the Messiah is again drawn to the foreground. In this case Micah is referring to the ancient promise made to Judah, Balaam and David.

3. YAHWEH: The third title used for this coming leader is "Yahweh". Only the Messiah is Lord and King.

HE MESSIAH AS THE COMING RULER (MICAH 5:1-4)

"Now gather yourself in troops, O daughter of troops; he has laid siege against us; they will strike the judge of Israel with a rod on the cheek. But you, Bethlehem Ephrathah, though you are little among the thousands of Judah, yet out of you shall come forth to Me the One to be Ruler in Israel, whose goings forth are from of old, from everlasting." Therefore He shall give them up, until the time that she who is in labor has given birth; then the remnant of his brethren shall return to the children of Israel. And He shall stand and feed His flock in the strength of the Lord, in the majesty of the name of the Lord His God; and they shall abide, for now He shall be great to the ends of the earth; and this One shall be peace.

The messianic predictions of Micah that pyramid to the surprise announcement of a coming Ruler mount up in three stages.

1. Micah first envisions a day when the mountain of the house of the Lord will be established above the highest mountains.

2. The tower of David that lost its ancient dominion will recover its former position. Micah christens the Tower of the Flock as the emblem of the future kingdom for the new David who is to come.

3. The greatest stage in this build-up of messianic promises will be achieved when the predicted Ruler comes from Bethlehem in that future day.

Micah 4:11 undoubtedly points to that final eschatological battle to settle the so-called "Jewish Question" appearing in Ezekiel, Joel and Zechariah.

Now also many nations have gathered against you, who say, "Let her be defiled, and let our eye look upon Zion."

Zion is then told in 5:1 to marshal her troops; the great day of the Lord is on. God will give a son to the family from Bethlehem (Ephrathah). The ancient promise has been fulfilled. Messiah, the eternal Son of God, both human and divine, will come forth as the new David. His birth and coming will signal a new day for God's people.

CHAPTER 13
ISAIAH

Isaiah is one of the most prolific announcers of the Messiah in His times among the Old Testament prophets. Probably for this reason he has sometimes been called "the fifth Evangelist," along with Matthew, Mark, Luke and John. Here we will consider several of the messianic texts of Isaiah.

MESSIAH AS KING

Let's look first at the regal theme of the Messiah, first given to Judah, then reappearing over the centuries. In Isaiah it comes fully.

1. THE BRANCH OF THE LORD (ISA 4:2)

In that day the Branch of the LORD shall be beautiful and glorious; and the fruit of the earth shall be excellent and appealing for those of Israel who have escaped.

This botanical figure of speech first appears in the last words of David, *"Is not my house established with God?... Will He not bring to fruition [or cause to sprout, branch out] my salvation...* (2 Sam 23:5). What was a verb there becomes a proper noun in this beautiful description of the Messiah. The expression is given voice in the four gospels:

    A. The Branch of David: Jeremiah 23:5-6 (likened to Matthew's presentation of Jesus as the Davidic Messiah (Matt 1:1).

    B. My servant, the Branch: Zechariah 3:8 (likened to Mark's presentation of Jesus as the Servant (Mark 19:45).

    C. The man whose name is the Branch: Zechariah 6:12 (likened to Luke's presentation of Jesus in his manly and human aspects (Luke 23:47).

    D. The Branch of the Lord: Isaiah 4:2 (likened to John's presentation of Jesus as from God (John 20:31).

2. THE VIRGIN BIRTH (ISA 7:1-16)

Pekah, king of the northern tribes of Israel (Ephraim), had made alliance with Rezin, king of Aram (i.e. Syria). Now they would try to march against Judah with every intention of overthrowing her. King Ahaz, of Judah (i.e. the house of David), were worried to say the least. God then spoke to Ahaz, king of Judah, and gave him a sign that Pekah and Rezin would not prevail. This gives us one of our most cherished messianic prophecies in the Bible: "Behold, a virgin shall conceive and bear a Son, and shall call His name Immanuel, God with us" (Isa 7:19). Indeed, it is from His name,

Immanuel, that we have derived the name of this present writing: "God with Us."

> *Moreover the LORD spoke again to Ahaz, saying, "Ask a sign for yourself from the LORD your God; ask it either in the depth or in the height above." But Ahaz said, "I will not ask, nor will I test the LORD!" Then he said, "Hear now, O house of David! Is it a small thing for you to weary men, but will you weary my God also? Therefore the Lord Himself will give you a sign: Behold, the virgin shall conceive and bear a Son, and shall call His name Immanuel. Curds and honey He shall eat, that He may know to refuse the evil and choose the good. For before the Child shall know to refuse the evil and choose the good, the land that you dread will be forsaken by both her kings. (Isa 7:10-17).*

What an uproar there was when the translators of the RSV in 1945 (1952) rendered "virgin" as "young woman"! The NRSV (1989) did not correct this unfortunate translation choice, but the ESV, which was an evangelical revision of the RSV, did render Isaiah 7:14 as "virgin." The evidence for the proper translation as "virgin" is solid, especially since quoted in the New Testament (Matt 1:23).

3. THE WONDERFUL RULING SON (ISA 9:1-7)

The context here is the same as in Isaiah 7:1-16. The threats from Damascus allied with the Northern kingdom of Israel will come to an end. The prophecy has near significance as the alliance will not prevail over Judah, and even greater significance for its messianic prediction, the Light of the World (John 1:5). The male child promised through Eve, the patriarchs and David, is cause for rejoicing. The government will be on His shoulders, and his name will be called "Wonderful, Counselor, Mighty God, Everlasting Father, Prince of Peace." God will bring this to pass. The divine nature of this Child is made clear in this text. For us, the prophecy has its fulfillment both in the incarnation of Jesus Christ and in His second coming where Christ will rule over all the nations, a peaceable kingdom.

> *The people who walked in darkness have seen a great light; those who dwelt in the land of the shadow of death, upon them a light has shined. You have multiplied the nation and increased its joy; they rejoice before You According to the joy of harvest, as men rejoice when they divide the spoil. For You have broken the yoke of his burden and the staff of his shoulder, the rod of his oppressor, as in the day of Midian. For every warrior's sandal from the noisy battle, and garments rolled in blood, will be used for burning and fuel of fire. For unto us a Child is born, unto us a Son is given; and the government will be upon His shoulder. And His name will be called Wonderful, Counselor, Mighty God, Everlasting Father, Prince of Peace. Of the increase of His government and peace there will be no end, upon the throne of David and over His kingdom, to order it and establish it with judgment and justice from that time forward, even forever. The zeal of the LORD of hosts will perform this.*

4. THE REIGN OF JESSIE'S SON (ISA 11:1-16)

This root from Jesse will yield a branch which will become the coming reign of Messiah. God will reassemble His people Israel from all over the earth; Jews will return from Assyria, Ethiopia, Egypt, Iran, Iraq, Syria, Lebanon and "the islands of the sea." Israel will swoop down over the Gaza Strip (ancient Philistia) and will subjugate the people to the east of their nation (presumably those in the Golan Heights. They will also lay hands on the ancient territory of Edom, Moab and Ammon. God will make a path through the Euphrates River. The end of the ancient struggle, which extends into modern Israel, will be mind-boggling as Jesus reigns with a rod of iron.

> *There shall come forth a Rod from the stem of Jesse, and a Branch shall grow out of his roots. ...He shall strike the earth with the rod of His mouth, and with the breath of His lips He shall slay the wicked. ... "The wolf also shall dwell with the lamb, the leopard shall lie down with the young goat, the calf and the young lion and the fatling together; and a little child shall lead them. ..."And in that day there shall be a Root of Jesse, Who shall stand as a banner to the people for the Gentiles shall seek Him, and His resting place shall be glorious." It shall come to pass in that day that the Lord shall set His hand again the second time to recover the remnant of His people who are left, From Assyria and Egypt, from Pathros and Cush, from Elam and Shinar, from Hamath and the islands of the sea. He will set up a banner for the nations, and will assemble the outcasts of Israel, and gather together the dispersed of Judah from the four corners of the earth. ...They*

> shall fly down upon the shoulder of the Philistines toward the west; together they shall plunder the people of the East; they shall lay their hand on Edom and Moab; and the people of Ammon shall obey them. The LORD will utterly destroy the tongue of the Sea of Egypt; with His mighty wind He will shake His fist over the River, and strike it in the seven streams, and make men cross over dry-shod. There will be a highway for the remnant of His people who will be left from Assyria, as it was for Israel In the day that he came up from the land of Egypt.

Delightful here is the use of the Hebrew word *'nezer'* for "Branch" (rendered NZR) in Isaiah 11:1. Matthew borrows NZR in Matthew 2:23, where it appears as NaZaReth. Matthew must have had a twinkle in his eye as he set forth that pun, a literary device that the prophets loved to employ.[63] By assonance, 'nezer' became "Nazarene" in his assertion that this was a fulfillment of prophecy, and would especially have been recognized in the Aramaic in which Matthew may have first appeared. So, Matthew is not so much exegeting Isaiah as he is recognizing that the Aramaic comes very close to the Hebrew word for branch, *'nezer'*. In other places such as in Jeremiah and Zechariah "branch" is translated from the more common *'tsamach,'* not *'nezer.'*

MESSIAH AS SERVANT

1. THE SERVANT'S MISSION TO THE WORLD (ISA 42:1-7; 49:1-6)

> "Behold! My Servant whom I uphold, My Elect One in whom My soul delights! I have put My Spirit upon Him; He will bring forth justice to the Gentiles. He will not cry out, nor

raise His voice, nor cause His voice to be heard in the street. A bruised reed He will not break, and smoking flax He will not quench; He will bring forth justice for truth. He will not fail nor be discouraged, till He has established justice in the earth; and the coastlands shall wait for His law." Thus says God the LORD, *Who created the heavens and stretched them out, Who spread forth the earth and that which comes from it, Who gives breath to the people on it, And spirit to those who walk on it: "I, the* LORD, *have called You in righteousness, and will hold Your hand; I will keep You and give You as a covenant to the people, as a light to the Gentiles, to open blind eyes, to bring out prisoners from the prison, those who sit in darkness from the prison house* (Isaiah 42:1-7).

Through Isaiah God the Father is revealing what He intends to do. This reminds us of Isaiah's observation in Chapter 9, verse 7: "The zeal of the Lord of Hosts will perform this." He will uphold His Elect One in whom His soul delights. This immediately reminds one of the voice from heaven at the baptismal presentation of Jesus: "Behold, My beloved Son in whom I am well pleased" (recorded by the synoptic gospels, Matthew, Mark and Luke). As God who had become flesh to dwell among us, God was pleased to put His Spirit upon Jesus, named Him Yeshua (which is Joshua or Jesus) according to the angel of the Lord as spoken to Mary, and was pleased to keep and uphold Him. What is meant by "a covenant to the people"? This could be summarized by Romans 10:9-10, *"that if you confess with your mouth the Lord Jesus and believe in your heart that God has raised Him from the dead, you will be saved. For with the heart one believes unto righteousness, and with the mouth confession is made unto salvation."* Jesus, sent by the Father as a servant, will now bring light and justice to the Gentiles. He is Light, because all the earth must know the truth of Jesus. Darkness, because without the revelation of God in Christ Jesus, we are all blind and under the sentence of death. Justice, because the grace, the mercy of our Creator who paid the price by sending the Son to the cross, has redeemed whosoever would believe. Through Him we are set free from the prison of sin.

It is interesting to hear what the servant will not do. He will not cry out to save Himself, nor will He have any need to build Himself up in the eyes of people. Instead He will empty Himself (Greek 'kenosis'); being found in human form, He will take on the form of a servant (Phil 2:7).

While Isaiah 42:1-7 emphasizes the Gentiles, Isaiah 49:1-6 clarifies the servanthood of Christ to Jacob/Israel:

> *"Listen, O coastlands, to Me, and take heed, you peoples from afar! The LORD has called Me from the womb; From the matrix of My mother He has made mention of My name. And He has made My mouth like a sharp sword; In the shadow of His hand He has hidden Me, And made Me a polished shaft; In His quiver He has hidden Me." "And He said to me, You are My servant, O Israel, In whom I will be glorified.' Then I said, 'I have labored in vain, I have spent my strength for nothing and in vain; yet surely my just reward is with the LORD, and my work with my God.'" "And now the LORD says, Who formed Me from the womb to be His Servant, to bring Jacob back to Him, so that Israel is gathered to Him (For I shall be glorious in the eyes of the LORD, and My God shall be My strength), Indeed He says, 'It is too small a thing that You should be My Servant to raise up the tribes of Jacob, and to restore the preserved ones of Israel; I will also give You as a light to the Gentiles, that You should be My salvation to the ends of the earth.'"*

Here the Messiah is identified with Israel to bring salvation to the Gentiles while given purpose to restore or bring back to Himself the tribes of Jacob.

2. THE SERVANT'S HUMILIATION (ISA 50:4-9)

"The Lord GOD has given Me the tongue of the learned, That I should know how to speak a word in season to him who is weary. He awakens Me morning by morning, He awakens My ear To hear as the learned. The Lord GOD has opened My ear; And I was not rebellious, Nor did I turn away. I gave My back to those who struck Me, and My cheeks to those who plucked out the beard; I did not hide My face from shame and spitting. "For the Lord GOD will help Me; therefore I will not be disgraced; therefore I have set My face like a flint, And I know that I will not be ashamed. He is near who justifies Me; who will contend with Me? Let us stand together. Who is My adversary? Let him come near Me. Surely the Lord GOD will help Me; who is he who will condemn Me? Indeed they will all grow old like a garment; the moth will eat them up.

This passage first addresses the student-teacher relationship of the Servant. The New Testament simply says Joseph and Mary found Jesus sitting among the teachers, listening to them and asking them questions. And all who heard Him were amazed at His understanding and His answers. This passage says that Jesus was submissive to His parents. It then goes on to say that Jesus increased in wisdom and in stature and in favor with God and man (Luke 2:46-52). The Bible leaves little doubt that Jesus knew who He was. And, He knew what was coming, even the crucifixion. Even in Gethsemane, through His humanity uttered *"if it be possible, let this cup pass from Me; nevertheless not as I will, but as Thou wilt"*

(Matt 26:39). For He had "set His face like a flint" that He might give His life a ransom for many. God's Servant, His Messiah, will come out of the humility of the cross approved by God and triumphant in God's plan.

3. THE SERVANT'S ATONEMENT (ISA 52:13-53:12)

This Scripture was put skillfully into music by the messianic Jew, Marty Goetz:

> *Who has believed our report?*
> *To whom has the arm of the Lord been revealed?*
> *He grew up among us, a tender shoot,*
> *A root from dry ground, in Him no beauty we found.*
>
> *Scorned and rejected by men,*
> *A man of sorrows, acquainted with grief,*
> *Like one from whom men hide their faces,*
> *Not esteemed but denied, not desired but despised.*
>
>> *He was wounded for our transgressions,*
>> *He was bruised for our iniquities.*
>> *The chastisement for our peace fell on Him*
>> *And by His stripes we are healed.*
>
> *Like a sheep before shearers is silent,*
> *As a lamb led to slaughter he said not a word:*
> *Assigned a grave with the wicked,*
> *Though no evil He'd done, no deceit was on his tongue.*
>
> *All we like sheep have gone astray,*
> *Turned, ev'ryone to his own way.*

> *Our iniquity on Him was laid.*
> *Surely he has born our griefs and our sorrows.*
> *He has born our griefs and our sorrows*
>
> *He was wounded for our transgressions,*
> *He was bruised for our iniquities.*
> *The chastisement for our peace fell on Him*
> *And by His stripes we are healed.*[64]

Dr. Walter Kaiser has coined this the "summit of Old Testament prophetic literature" for its clarity on the suffering, death, burial and resurrection of the Messiah. The death of the Servant is no misadventure or accident; it is the deliberate plan and will of God.[65] It is no wonder that John's Revelation sees the Messiah as the One *worthy to receive power and wealth and wisdom and might and honor and glory and blessing* (Rev 5:12).

MESSIAH AS THE CONSUMMATION OF ALL THINGS

1. MESSIAH AS HEALER (ISA 35:5-6)

The eyes of the blind shall be opened, and the ears of the deaf shall be unstopped. Then the lame shall leap like a deer, and the tongue of the dumb sing.

2. MESSIAH AS COMFORTER (ISA 40:1-11)

Handel's oratorio, The Messiah, begins with the announcement from Isaiah 40, the tenor recitative and air *"Comfort ye, comfort ye my people, saith your God. Speak ye comfortably to Jerusalem, and cry unto her, that her warfare is accomplished, that her iniquity is pardoned.*

The voice of him that crieth in the wilderness; prepare ye the way of the Lord; make straight in the desert a highway for our God. Every valley shall be exalted, and every mountain and hill made low; the crooked straight, and the rough places plain."

The chorus follows with *"And the glory of the Lord shall be revealed, and all flesh shall see it together, for the mouth of the Lord hath spoken it."*

The alto air and chorus follows with *"O thou that tellest good tidings to Zion, get thee up into the high mountain. O thou that tellest good tidings to Jerusalem, lift up they voice with strength; lift it up, be not afraid; say unto the cities of Judah, behold your God! O thou that tellest good tidings to Zion, Arise, shine, for thy Light is come, and the glory of the Lord is risen upon thee."*

Later the soprano aria interprets Isaiah's characterization of this conquering Messiah: "He shall feed His flock like a shepherd; and He shall gather the lambs with His arm, and carry them in His bosom, and gently lead those that are with young. Come unto Him, all ye that labor, come unto Him that are heavy laden, and he will give you rest."

This is followed by Jesus' words in Matthew 11:28-29: "Come unto Him, all ye that labor, come unto Him that are heavy laden, and He will give you rest. Take His yoke upon you, and learn of Him, for he is meek and lowly of heart, and ye shall find rest unto your souls."

3. MESSIAH AS A GIFT TO ALL NATIONS (ISA 55:3-5)

Incline your ear, and come to Me. Hear, and your soul shall live; And I will make an everlasting covenant with you— the sure mercies of David. Indeed I have given him as a witness to the people, a leader and commander for the people. Surely you shall call a nation you do not know, And nations who do not know you shall run to you, because of the LORD your God, And the Holy One of Israel; for He has glorified you."

When Paul and Barnabas came to Antioch to a synagogue of the Jews, Isaiah's prophecy was quoted in part: *"I will give you the holy and sure blessings of David"* (Acts 13:34b). As they announced that this good news from Isaiah and the Psalms had been fulfilled in Jesus, many people begged that they return the following Sabbath to show them more. So they did. The gift given also to the Gentiles is expressed as *"a nation you do not know, and nations who do not know you shall run to you."* *"A leader and commander for the people"* is reference to the Messiah as giver of the commandments and teacher.

4. MESSIAH AS PROCLAIMER (ISA 61:1-3)

"The Spirit of the Lord GOD is upon Me, Because the LORD has anointed Me To preach good tidings to the poor; He has sent Me to heal the brokenhearted, to proclaim liberty to the captives, And the opening of the prison to those who are bound; to proclaim the acceptable year of the LORD, And the day of vengeance of our God; to comfort all who mourn, to console those who mourn in Zion, to give them beauty for ashes, the oil of joy for mourning, The garment of praise for the spirit of heaviness; that they may be called trees of righteousness, the planting of the LORD, that He may be glorified."

This is the passage that Jesus read in the synagogue, after which He rolled up the scroll, sat down and said, *"Today this Scripture has been fulfilled in your hearing"* (Luke 4:18-21).

5. MESSIAH AS CONQUEROR (ISA 63:1-6)

Who is this who comes from Edom, with dyed garments from Bozrah, this One who is glorious in His apparel, Traveling in the greatness of His strength?— "I who speak in righteousness, mighty to save." Why is Your apparel red, And Your garments like one who treads in the winepress? "I have trodden the winepress alone, and from the peoples no one was with Me. For I have trodden them in My anger, and trampled them in My fury; their blood is sprinkled upon My garments, and I have stained all My robes. For the day of vengeance is in My heart, And the year of My redeemed has come. I looked, but there was no one to help, And I wondered that there was no one to uphold; therefore My own arm brought salvation for Me; and My own fury, it sustained Me. I have trodden down the peoples in My anger, made them drunk in My fury, And brought down their strength to the earth."

Edom here is an archetype for the Lord's enemies, "the people I have devoted to destruction" (Isa 34:5). This allusion to the second advent of Christ can be seen in John's Revelation 19:11-21 where he sees the utter destruction from the "Rider on a White Horse who is called "Faithful and True." He is clothed in a robe dipped in blood. He is leading the armies of heaven. The beast and the false prophet are thrown alive into the lake of fire and the rest are slain by the sword that comes from the mouth of Him who was sitting on the horse. This work of wrath on "the day of vengeance" will conquer all that is evil. The Messiah will be the judge, jury and executioner of all the earth.

CHAPTER 14
SEVENTH & SIXTH CENTURY PROPHETS

JEREMIAH

God called Jeremiah when he was still a teenager in the era of King Josiah's national revival. There were great hopes that the people would repent and that the gains of Josiah would be preserved. However, that is not the way it turned out. Not only were the words of Jeremiah rejected, Jeremiah suffered great abuse for his preaching. He is often called "the weeping prophet" who wrote The Lamentations. But, God was faithful to him and placed within him a future and a hope for the Jewish remnant who believed.

1. MESSIAH AS THE LORD OF OUR RIGHTEOUSNESS (JER 23:5-6)

"Behold, the days are coming," says the LORD, *"That I will raise to David a Branch of righteousness; A King shall reign and prosper, and execute judgment and righteousness in the earth. In His days Judah will be saved, And Israel will dwell safely; now this is His name by which He will be called: THE LORD OUR RIGHTEOUSNESS.*

In the messianic age following the second coming of Jesus Christ, He will rule according to the promise given to David of an eternal kingdom. The Christian church has been appealing to this passage for centuries to demonstrate the deity of Jesus. The Lord our Righteousness is rendered as an appositive rather than as "the Lord is our righteousness" as with the RSV, ESV, CEB and NLT bibles. Their argument for this rendering is that Jeremiah is playing on the name Zedekiah which means "the Lord is my righteousness." Of course Zedekiah was the last king of Judah, and if the promise to David was to be kept, and if there is to be a branch from David as already discussed in Isaiah 4:2, then it will be "in that day" or "the days coming."

2. MESSIAH AS THE PRIESTLY KING (JER 30:9,21)

But they shall serve the LORD *their God, and David their king, whom I will raise up for them. Their nobles shall be from among them, and their governor shall come from their midst; Then I will cause Him to draw near, and He shall approach Me; For who is this who pledged his heart to approach Me?' says the* LORD.

Jeremiah's so-called Book of Comfort (Jer 30-33) contains some of the finest statements on what God is going to do in the future day. Of course, Chapter 31 announces the "new covenant." In 30:9 it is clear that the Lord will raise up "David their king" in the line of David. This is their Messiah, called the "new David" in Eze 34:23; 37:24; and Hos 3:5. The first David may have liberated the nation from the Philistines, but the second David will free the nation from tyranny that will be far greater than David ever witnessed. God will raise up this king Messiah to carry out this final work of judgment and adjudication. That "He shall approach Me" indicates the priestly role of Messiah.

3. THE INVIOLABLE PROMISE ABOUT THE MESSIAH (JER 33:14-26)

'Behold, the days are coming,' says the LORD, 'that I will perform that good thing which I have promised to the house of Israel and to the house of Judah: 'In those days and at that time will cause to grow up to David a Branch of righteousness; he shall execute judgment and righteousness in the earth. In those days Judah will be saved, and Jerusalem will dwell safely. And this is the name by which she will be called: THE LORD OUR RIGHTEOUSNESS.' (Jer 33:14-16)

Here is repeated the prediction of Jeremiah 23:5-6 which we have already discussed above. The days are coming when God will fulfill the promise He made to Israel and Judah. But, here in the last chapter of Jeremiah's Book of Comfort is added more information:

> "For thus says the LORD: 'David shall never lack a man to sit on the throne of the house of Israel; nor shall the priests, the Levites, lack a man to offer burnt offerings before Me, to kindle grain offerings, and to sacrifice continually.'" (Jer 33:17-18)

Just as David will never lack a man to sit on his throne forever, so the priests and the Levites, who serve at the altar and in God's house of worship, will never be without representatives to fulfill this function. In the following verses is described the fact that the word of the Lord regarding this matter can no more be broken than God's covenant with day and night. From our modern point of view that involves the rotation of the earth. Despite the captivity of the Assyrians and Babylonians, though temples were destroyed, Jews harassed, local populations of Jews killed, ethnic cleansing practiced, Hitler could not have been successful in the holocaust and none of these ultimately successful:

> As the host of heaven cannot be numbered, nor the sand of the sea measured, so will I multiply the descendants of David My servant and the Levites who minister to Me.'"

Even though God allows calamity to come on the children of Israel, He assures them that He will never cast off the "two families which the Lord has chosen," that of Jacob and of David. Not only will He bring them back from captivity in God's mercy, but there will be an eternal king in the line of David.

EZEKIEL

Ezekiel a younger contemporary of Jeremiah was carried off into captivity in 598 B.C. along with Daniel and many other of the young best educated citizens of Judea. There he ministered to the captive

Jews. In his book he proclaims five direct prophecies of the Messiah found in four passages:

1. MESSIAH AS THE TENDER SHOOT (EZE 17:22-24)

> *Thus says the Lord GOD: "I will take also one of the highest branches of the high cedar and set it out. I will crop off from the topmost of its young twigs a tender one, and will plant it on a high and prominent mountain. On the mountain height of Israel I will plant it; and it will bring forth boughs, and bear fruit, and be a majestic cedar. Under it will dwell birds of every sort; in the shadow of its branches they will dwell. And all the trees of the field shall know that I, the LORD, have brought down the high tree and exalted the low tree, dried up the green tree and made the dry tree flourish; I, the LORD, have spoken and have done it."*

In this allegory the tender shoot is, of course, from the house of David, the Messiah. The growth of the tender shoot will be sensational. "It will produce branches and bear fruit and become a splendid cedar." The kingdom of the Messiah will be as stately as the cedar tree itself. The tree will also be a nesting place for "birds of every kind." Presumably the birds represent people from all the nations of the earth. So spectacular will be the growth of the cedar tree (i.e. the kingdom of the Messiah) that "all the trees of the field will know that I the Lord bring down the tall tree and make the low tree grow tall." In other words, the royal house of David, of which the Messiah will be the climax, will so outstrip all the royal trees of the earth that all other sovereignties will have to acknowledge that the growth of this tender shoot simply must be the work of God. What was the tree (the Davidic line) will flourish by the power of the promise-plan of God, and the green trees (all the governments of the world) will dry up under the condescension and judgment of the living God. The shoot of David, the Messiah's rule and reign, will grow and prosper for all eternity.⁶⁶

2. MESSIAH AS THE RIGHTFUL KING (EZE 21:25-27)

'Now to you, O profane, wicked prince of Israel, whose day has come, whose iniquity shall end, thus says the Lord GOD: "Remove the turban, and take off the crown; Nothing shall remain the same. Exalt the humble, and humble the exalted. Overthrown, overthrown, I will make it overthrown! It shall be no longer, Until He comes whose right it is, and I will give it to Him."'

Babylon had carried King Jehoiachin into captivity and installed Zedekiah as king of Judah. Zedekiah does not consider God, acts foolishly in his overtures toward Egypt intending to become allied to them and has his troops slain by the Babylonians. Ezekiel addresses this profane, wicked king whose day has come. "Remove the turban and take off the crown" refer to both priestly and kingly roles. Thus, the kingdom and priesthood, as experienced up to that point in Israel's history, will be removed and abolished, suffering an interruption for a period of time. "I will make it a ruin," declares the Lord, "until He comes whose right it is, and I will give it to Him." The Messiah will be the final King-Priest.

3. MESSIAH AS THE GOOD SHEPHERD (EZE 34:23-31)

"I will establish one shepherd over them, and he shall feed them—My servant David. He shall feed them and be their shepherd. And I, the LORD, will be their God, and My servant David a prince among them; I, the LORD, have spoken. I will make a covenant of peace with them, and cause wild beasts to cease from the land; and they will dwell safely in the wilderness and sleep in the woods. I will make them and the places all around My hill a blessing; and I will cause showers to come down in their season; there shall be showers of blessing. Then the trees of the field shall yield their fruit, and the earth shall yield her increase. They shall be safe in their land; and they shall know that I am the LORD, when I have broken the bands of their yoke and delivered them from the hand of those who enslaved them. And they shall no longer be a prey for the nations, nor shall beasts of the land devour them; but they shall dwell safely, and no one shall make them afraid. I will raise up for them a garden of renown, and they shall no longer be consumed with hunger in the land, nor bear the shame of the Gentiles anymore. Thus they shall know that I, the LORD their God, am with them, and they, the house of Israel, are My people," says the Lord GOD. *"You are My flock, the flock of My pasture; you are men, and I am your God,"* says the Lord GOD.

This passage begins with a prophecy similar to that of Isaiah: "He shall feed His flock like a shepherd: He shall gather the lambs with His arm, and carry them in His bosom" (Isa 40:11). The same figure of the tender Shepherd appears in Psalms 78:52-53, 79:13 and 80:1. Jerusalem has fallen, and now Ezekiel gives his attention to what God will yet do in spite of human failures. He turns to discuss the last days, when Yahweh will wrap up the historical process. God will raise up a Shepherd. He will be the God of His people. This Shepherd will be a ruling and reigning prince in the line of David. At last Judah will find the rest she has longed for throughout her history. This will only happen when the Messiah returns again, the Second Coming of the Lord. Here is a covenant of peace paralleling Jeremiah's "new covenant." The physical and spiritual aspects of this covenant of peace are simultaneous, and it is not only for Israel but for the whole world.

4. MESSIAH AS THE GREAT UNIFIER OF THE NATION (EZE 37:15-28)

Then say to them, "Thus says the Lord GOD: Surely I will take the children of Israel from among the nations, wherever they have gone, and will gather them from every side and bring them into their own land; and I will make them one nation in the land, on the mountains of Israel; and one king shall be king over them all; they shall no longer be two nations, nor shall they ever be divided into two kingdoms again. They shall not defile themselves anymore with their idols, nor with their detestable things, nor with any of their transgressions; but I will deliver them from all their dwelling places in which they have sinned, and will cleanse them. Then they shall be My people, and I will be their God" (Eze 37:21-23).

It is apparent that this prophecy is, at least, partially fulfilled with the 1948 establishment of Israel as a nation. Although they are generally a secular state in their practice of freedom of religion, there has been a public acknowledgement of the protection of God over their little nation. They are still concerned with the ancient Jewish mission of being a light unto the nations. The simple fact is that no one is in charge of the Jewish People world-wide, even though the Jewish state exists for all the Jews of the world. Jews have no president, prime minister or king. Even in Israel the prime minister is not to be considered as king of the Jews, but rather their servant. They are organized as a decentralized network of communities that have multiple centers of power, which compete over leadership and influence. Prime Minister Benjamin Netanyahu has a family Bible study every Sabbath in his home. In addition he has revived a tradition of Bible study hosted at His home which was started by David Ben-Gurion, Israel's first prime minister. Golda Meir, Moshe Dayan, Menachem Begin and the several prime ministers of Israel have been concerned with Zionism, the return from Diaspora of Jews to the land God has given them. Yet, one sees from the text above that the ingathering will be more complete in the future, for there will be a cleansing from sin and a complete turning to God that has not yet taken place.

> *"David My servant shall be king over them, and they shall all have one shepherd; they shall also walk in My judgments and observe My statutes, and do them. Then they shall dwell in the land that I have given to Jacob My servant, where your fathers dwelt; and they shall dwell there, they, their children, and their children's children, forever; and My servant David shall be their prince forever. Moreover I will make a covenant of peace with them, and it shall be an everlasting covenant with them; I will establish them and multiply them, and I will set My sanctuary in their midst forevermore. My tabernacle also shall be with them; indeed I will be their God, and they shall be*

My people. The nations also will know that I, the LORD, sanctify Israel, when My sanctuary is in their midst forevermore"(Eze 37:24-28).

The missing person in the completion of Israel is the Messiah. He came to His own, and they did not know Him. But He is coming again, will "be their Prince forever" AND will "sanctify Israel and make a sanctuary in their midst." Moreover, all the nations will know it.

DANIEL

Like Ezekiel, Daniel was carried away to captivity as a young man. Like Joseph in Egypt and Esther in Persia, Daniel with God's help rose to the top as he served over some seventy years in Babylon and Medo-Persia. Two passages in Daniel speak directly of the Messiah and his coming, even though much of what he says pertains to the messianic times:

MESSIAH AS THE SON OF MAN (DAN 7:13-14)

> "I was watching in the night visions, And behold, one like the Son of Man, Coming with the clouds of heaven! He came to the Ancient of Days, and they brought Him near before Him. Then to Him was given dominion and glory and a kingdom, that all peoples, nations, and languages should serve Him. His dominion is an everlasting dominion, which shall not pass away, and His kingdom the one which shall not be destroyed.

In Daniel's vision God shows him the rise and fall of four successive kingdoms: Babylon, Medo-Persia, Greece and Rome.

Suddenly he sees "the Ancient of Days" (i.e. God the Father) take His seat on a throne, flaming with fire. His clothing was white as snow; the hair of his head was white like wool" "A river of fire was flowing" forth from in front of Him as "thousands upon thousands attended him" and "ten thousand time ten thousand stood before Him." It is an awesome sight as the God of the universe moves to render worldwide judgment while receiving the praise of millions of the redeemed who are already at home in His presence and who await the climactic event of history. But the most significant person who comes before him is "one like a son of man." This "son of man" is another messianic title, for He is a human being. Furthermore "all rulers will worship Him; He is therefore also divine. Also, that He comes from "the clouds of heaven" suggests His divine origin. This "son of man" will have an eternal dominion, unequaled glory and splendor without rival.

MESSIAH AS THE ANNOINTED RULER WHO WILL COME (DAN 9:24-27)

> *"Seventy weeks are determined for your people and for your holy city, to finish the transgression, to make an end of sins, to make reconciliation for iniquity, to bring in everlasting righteousness, to seal up vision and prophecy, And to anoint the Most Holy. "Know therefore and understand, that from the going forth of the command to restore and build Jerusalem Until Messiah the Prince, there shall be seven weeks and sixty-two weeks; the street shall be built again, and the wall, even in troublesome times. "And after the sixty-two weeks Messiah shall be cut off, but not for Himself; and the people of the prince who is to come shall destroy the city and the sanctuary. The end of it shall be with a flood, and till the end of the war*

desolations are determined. Then he shall confirm a covenant with many for one week; but in the middle of the week He shall bring an end to sacrifice and offering. And on the wing of abominations shall be one who makes desolate, even until the consummation, which is determined, is poured out on the desolate."

Some have commented that Daniel's "seventy weeks of seven" is the key to understanding all eschatology. Out of this six things will be accomplished:

1. "finish transgression,"
2. "put an end to sin,"
3. "atone for wickedness,"
4. "bring in everlasting righteousness,"
5. "seal up vison and prophecy," and
6. "anoint the most holy One."

For our purpose here we will highlight only the Messiah reference of this passage. Suffice to say that there is coming an end to transgression (to sin), there is going to be a reconciliation and there will be ushered in everlasting righteousness. Daniel saw an end to vision and prophecy and the anointing of Messiah the Prince. There will be a tribulation period where God's judgment will sweep over the earth; "and on the wing of abominations shall be One who makes desolate." Out of judgment will be the consummation of all things, and Messiah will be made king of kings and Lord of lords forever.

CHAPTER 15
POST EXILIC PROPHETS

The decree of Cyrus, king of Medo-Persia, permitted the Jewish people to return to their own land and to rebuild the temple (Ezra 1:2-4). The wall of Jerusalem had been built under the leadership of Nehemiah and a revival of the people was directed under Ezra. Zerubbabel (from the house of David) and Joshua, the high priest, lead the people to rebuild the temple. Soon they became discouraged, and the reconstruction lay dormant from 536 to 516 B.C. Then God raised up two prophets, Haggai and Zechariah, to stir up the hearts and resolve of the people to return to the project.

HAGGAI

MESSIAH AS DESIRE OF ALL NATIONS (HAG 2:6-9)

> *"For thus says the L*ORD *of hosts: 'Once more (it is a little while) I will shake heaven and earth, the sea and dry land; and I will shake all nations, and they shall come to the Desire of All Nations, and I will fill this temple with glory,' says the L*ORD *of hosts. 'The silver is Mine, and the gold is Mine,' says the L*ORD *of hosts. 'The glory of this latter temple shall be greater than the former,' says the L*ORD *of hosts. 'And in this place I will give peace,' says the L*ORD *of hosts."(NKJV)*

In the last day there will be a worldwide shake-up that will signal the final appearance of Christ as He comes to reign forever. For the technical argument as to the rendering of the Hebrew word translated "Desire," see Dr. Kaiser.[67] Some modern versions, e.g. ASV, RSV, NEB, HCSB and NASB, translate this word "precious things," "wealth" or "treasurer" which changes the meaning altogether. The NIV compromises with the rendering, "and what is desired by all nations will come." If we agree with Dr. Kaiser and others in the KJV or NKJV rendering, "the Desire of all Nations" is messianic. It would make sense that only with Christ's second coming will there be shaking as described in the book of Revelation and a glorious temple be built (whether that be a tribulation temple or a millennial temple). Only then will there be peace given by the Lord of hosts and the temple be filled with the glory of God.

ZECHARIAH

Zechariah's book is not only the longest of the twelve minor prophets, it is one of the most frequently quoted Old Testament books in the New Testament (seventy-one quotations or allusions). Zechariah is second only to Ezekiel in its influence on the book of Revelation. His prophecies both advance the doctrine of the Messiah and summarize the previous promises made about the coming son of David.

In Zechariah's vision (Zech 3:1-7) Satan accuses Joshua, who appears in priestly robes that are dung-spattered (representing the filthiness of sin). But the "Angel of the Lord," who is no doubt a pre-incarnate form of Christ, orders the foul clothes to be removed from Joshua. The Lord then recommissions Joshua, the high priest, and grants him direct access to God the Father.

MESSIAH'S WORK AS HIGH PRIEST (ZECH 3:8-10)

> "...'Hear, O Joshua, the high priest, you and your companions who sit before you, for they are a wondrous sign; for behold, I am bringing forth My Servant the BRANCH. For behold, the stone that I have laid before Joshua: Upon the stone are seven eyes. Behold, I will engrave its inscription,' Says the LORD of hosts, 'and I will remove the iniquity of that land in one day. In that day,' says the LORD of hosts, 'everyone will invite his neighbor under his vine and under his fig tree.'"

Coincidentally, the high priest Joshua (Yeshua) has the same name, when translated into Greek, as Jesus. Two marvelous titles of the Messiah appear in the last part of verse 8: "my servant" and "the Branch." There is a third messianic title in this text, that of "Stone." It was announced in Psalm 118:22 as the Chief Cornerstone that the builders rejected. The cleansing of "that land in one day" looks forward to the accomplishment of the Messiah on Calvary. The vision of tranquility and rest, since each sin has been pardoned and removed, in which everyone sits under his own vine and fig tree, is a reference to the future age when the Messiah reigns supreme without any rivals.

MESSIAH AS KING-PRIEST: RULER OF THE NATIONS (ZECH 6:9-15)

> Then the word of the LORD came to me, saying: "Receive the gift from the captives—from Heldai, Tobijah, and Jedaiah, who have come from Babylon—and go the same day and enter the house of Josiah the son of Zephaniah. Take the silver and gold, make an elaborate crown, and set it on the

> head of Joshua the son of Jehozadak, the high priest. Then speak to him, saying, 'Thus says the LORD of hosts, saying: "Behold, the Man whose name is the BRANCH! From His place He shall branch out, And He shall build the temple of the LORD; yes, He shall build the temple of the LORD. He shall bear the glory, and shall sit and rule on His throne; So He shall be a priest on His throne, and the counsel of peace shall be between them both."' "Now the elaborate crown shall be for a memorial in the temple of the LORD for Helem, Tobijah, Jedaiah, and Hen the son of Zephaniah. Even those from afar shall come and build the temple of the LORD. Then you shall know that the LORD of hosts has sent Me to you. And this shall come to pass if you diligently obey the voice of the LORD your God."

David Baron has remarked concerning this passage: "This is one of the most remarkable and precious messianic prophecies, and there is no plainer prophetic utterance in the whole OT as to the Person of the promised Redeemer, the offices He was to fill, and the mission He was to accomplish."[68]

The kingly crown to be placed on the head of Joshua, the high priest, represented the dual role of the Messiah as priest and king. The ceremony was to be followed by the prophecy "Behold, the Man whose name is the Branch!" The announcement is made that there will be a Davidic king who will come in the new age of God who will be from human stock, yet He will have the title of "Branch." Secondly, "He will branch out from His place." Born in lowly Bethlehem (a root from dry ground) God will exalt, elevate and prosper the Messiah in accordance with His own nature. Thirdly, He will "build the temple of the Lord." All the splendor that the glory and honor of His position affords Him will belong to Messiah in that day, and this will be observable by all (Psa 96:6). Fourthly,

He "will sit and rule on His throne." This is the promise made to David long ago (2 Sam 7:12-16). Finally, "He will be a priest on His throne, and there will be harmony between the two." This is a clear statement that the Messiah will be both a king and priest resolving the tension between the offices of the religious and political leadership.

MESSIAH AS KING (ZECH 9:9-10)

> *"Rejoice greatly, O daughter of Zion! Shout, O daughter of Jerusalem! Behold, your King is coming to you; He is just and having salvation, Lowly and riding on a donkey, a colt, the foal of a donkey. I will cut off the chariot from Ephraim and the horse from Jerusalem; the battle bow shall be cut off. He shall speak peace to the nations; His dominion shall be 'from sea to sea, and from the River to the ends of the earth.'*

Here we recognize the specific detail fulfilled in Jesus' triumphal entry into Jerusalem on a colt as detailed in all four gospels (Matt 21:1-17; Mark 11:1-11; Luke 19:19-49; John 12:12-19). Here four announcements are made: that spontaneous outbursts of exuberant joy break out in an enormous celebration over the fact that the earth will finally receive her king; that the character of Messiah is described as righteous and having salvation; that the world will be disarmed and; that the Messiah "will proclaim peace to the nations." The scope of Messiah's realm will be from "sea to sea and from the River to the ends of the earth."

MESSIAH'S FOUR TITLES (ZECH 10:4)

From Him comes the cornerstone, from Him the tent peg, from Him the battle bow, from Him every ruler together.

1. **Cornerstone:** The Messiah will be the foundation and the unifier of the people who belong to Him by right of redemption. The term cornerstone also appeared above in Isaiah 28:16 to refer to the Messiah as the Stone that human beings rejected, but which eventually became the cornerstone. The Messiah became "the cornerstone" in Psalm 118:22 (Matt 21:42). This metaphor depicts steadfastness, reliability and headship.

2. **Tent Peg:** Isaiah declared in Isaiah 22:22-23 (reflected in Rev 3:7) that God would "drive him like a peg into a firm place," for God had placed on Eliakim's shoulder "the key to the house of David" so that "what he opens no one can shut, and what he shuts no one can open." So, Eliakim, a son of David, emerged as another in the line of the Messiah. Accordingly, the Messiah will be the Nail in a sure place on whom his people can hang all their burdens, cares and anxieties.

3. **The Battle-Bow:** This is a symbol of strength for military conquests. This character is given to the Messiah in Psalm 110:5-6 and in Isaiah 63 (as reflected in Revelation 19). When the Messiah comes, He will be like a sharp sword in the hand of the Almighty, for He will smite the nations who have by then filled up the cup of iniquity. He will rule them with a rod of iron and dash them in pieces like a potter's vessel (Psalm 2:9).

4. **Absolute Ruler:** above all of them, "every ruler together."

MESSIAH AS REJECTED GOOD SHEPHERD (ZECH 11:4-14)

This is what the LORD my God says: "Shepherd the flock marked for slaughter. Their buyers slaughter them and go unpunished. Those who sell them say, 'Praise the LORD, I am rich!' Their own shepherds do not spare them. For I will no longer have pity on the people of the land," declares the LORD. "I will give everyone into the hands of their neighbors and their king. They will devastate the land, and I will not rescue anyone from their hands." So I shepherded the flock marked for slaughter, particularly the oppressed of the flock. Then I took two staffs and called one Favor and the other Union, and I shepherded the flock. In one month I got rid of the three shepherds. The flock detested me, and I grew weary of them and said, "I will not be your shepherd. Let the dying die, and the perishing perish. Let those who are left eat one another's flesh." Then I took my staff called Favor and broke it, revoking the covenant I had made with all the nations. It was revoked on that day, and so the oppressed of the flock who were watching me knew it was the word of the LORD. I told them, "If you think it best, give me my pay; but if not, keep it." So they paid me thirty pieces of silver. And the LORD said to me, "Throw it to the potter"—the handsome price at which they valued me! So I took the thirty pieces of silver and threw them to the potter at the house of the LORD. Then I broke my second staff called Union, breaking the family bond between Judah and Israel. (NIV)

Here God tells Zechariah to act out a kind of parable prophesying God's attitude toward Judah/Israel as exemplified in the poor shepherding of the sheep. While it is uncertain, the three shepherds may represent the chief priest, scribes and elders of the Jews or the contemporary kings, priests and false prophets. The picture here is of the shepherd(s) of Israel who, because of their neglect of the people, have been left open to abuse by others who have slaughtered the people without feeling of guilt. Seeing that Israel's own shepherds will have no pity and in effect abandon God's flock for motives of profiteering, God Himself will abandon them in the future and hand the whole land over to Israel's neighbors and to foreign kings as the prize of conquest. Zechariah, with "Favor" and "Union" depicts the shepherd who influences the reuniting of Northern and Southern kingdoms. But Zechariah, as the shepherd is rejected by the people, breaks the staff called "Favor" thereby revoking the covenant that God made with all the nations (that God would protect Israel by keeping the nations at bay). Zechariah cast away the thirty pieces of silver paid to him (which looks forward to Judas' guilt-ridden act of throwing the 30 pieces of silver, paid him by the Jewish leaders to lead them to Jesus, onto the temple floor). Then Zechariah broke his staff "Union" that the brotherhood between Judah and Israel be severed. The strong messianic prophecy obviously is the rejected Good Shepherd.

MESSIAH AS THE PIERCED ONE (ZECH 12:10)

> "And I will pour on the house of David and on the inhabitants of Jerusalem the Spirit of grace and supplication; then they will look on Me whom they pierced. Yes, they will mourn for Him as one mourns for his only son, and grieve for Him as one grieves for a firstborn.

Since it is impossible to pierce God since He is not flesh and blood, the pronoun *'Me'* must have the same referent as "they will mourn for *'Him'*." Since Zechariah has just referred to the Good Shepherd being rejected by Israel in Chapter 11, the context supports this interpretation. Only the character and person of the Messiah fits all the details given here. The prediction of the Messiah's death on the cross and His being literally pierced is another startling fulfillment of prophecy. There will be a tremendous period of national grief which will take place when Israel realizes one day that the Pierced One who died on the cross on Golgotha was the Messiah and that He died for their sins as well as for the sins of the whole world (Isa 53:5).

MESSIAH AS SMITTEN COMPANION OF THE LORD (ZECH 13:7)

"Awake, O sword, against My Shepherd, against the Man who is My Companion," says the LORD *of hosts. "Strike the Shepherd, and the sheep will be scattered; then I will turn My hand against the little ones.*

Here the Lord was pleased (Isa 53:10a) to bruise or crush the One described as "My Shepherd." The Shepherd who is struck by the sword in Zechariah 13:7 is obviously the same as the one described as being pierced in 12:10 and as being rejected in Chapter 11. Once again, this messianic prophecy is speaking about a human being "the Man," who is also divine (He is "close to Me"). When the messianic shepherd is smitten, the sheep "will be scattered." In other words, following the death of the Messiah, the dispersion of the Jews around the world took place, and particularly after the destruction of the temple in AD 70. The tradition of resisting the divine implications of the hideous death of the Messiah, however, has been passed on from Jewish parents to their "little ones." And so the opposition to His person and work has continued to this day.

MALACHI

MESSIAH AS MESSENGER OF THE COVENANT (MAL 3:1-3)

> *"Behold, I send My messenger, and he will prepare the way before Me. And the Lord, whom you seek, will suddenly come to His temple, even the Messenger of the covenant, in whom you delight. Behold, He is coming," says the* LORD *of hosts. But who can endure the day of his coming? And who can stand when He appears? For He is like a refiner's fire and like launderers' soap. He will sit as a refiner and a purifier of silver; He will purify the sons of Levi, and purge them as gold and silver, that they may offer to the Lord an offering in righteousness.*

This strong messianic passage begins with reference to John the Baptist who was foretold in Isa 40:3-5. He would come in the spirit and power of Elijah, and his job would be to prepare the people morally and spiritually for the coming of the Messiah. Then "the Lord, whom you seek, will suddenly come to His temple." This was fulfilled in the episode with Simeon and Ana (Luke 2:21-40): *"My eyes have seen Your salvation, which You have prepared in the sight of all nations: a light for revelation to the Gentiles, and the glory of Your people*

Israel." The Messiah will be "the Messenger of the covenant and purifier."

MESSIAH AS SUN OF RIGHTEOUSNESS (MAL 4:2)

But to you who fear My name, the Sun of Righteousness shall arise with healing in His wings; and you shall go out and grow fat like stall-fed calves.

The title "sun of righteousness" is a messianic title, for it has roots in the previous revelations about the Messiah. It is connected with the star that will come out of Jacob (Num 24:17), the great light that will arise in Zebulun and Naphtali (Isa 9:2), and the light that will be for all the Gentiles to see (Isa 42:6: 49:6). Jeremiah called the Messiah "the Lord Our Righteousness" (Jer 23:5-6; 33:15-16). In the New Testament another priest named Zechariah would bless the infant John the Baptist and blend together Malachi 4:2 with Isaiah 9:2 in Luke 1:76-79:

"And You, child, will be called the prophet of the Most High; for you will go before the Lord to prepare His ways, to give knowledge of salvation to His people in the forgiveness of their sins, because of the tender mercy of our God, whereby the sunrise shall visit us from on high to give light to those who sit in darkness and in the shadow of death, to guide our feet into the way of peace."

This would signal a whole new day for God's people. On that day they will break out into exuberant joy, like calves released for the first time in the spring of the year (Micah 2:12-13). It will signal a day when the Messiah's victory over all evil-doers will be complete (Mal 4:3). The wicked will be trampled under foot as ashes on the soles of the Messiah's feet. His will be the kingdom and the glory and the power forever and ever.[69]

CHAPTER 16
CONCLUSION

The Messiah, the Messenger of the covenant, is the "consummation of Israel." The covenant indicated here is the single plan of God contained in the succession of covenants that began with the word issued to Eve in Genesis 3:15, continued in the word given to Shem in Genesis 9:27, to Abraham in Genesis 12:2-3, to David in 2 Samuel 7:12-19, and  renewed and enlarged in Jeremiah 31:31-34. This Messenger of the covenant is the same person God sent ahead of Israel as they left Egypt (Exod 23:20-23), in whom Yahweh placed his own "Name" (Exod 23:21). There can be no mistaking His identity, for to equate the name of God with His angel or messenger is to call Him divine!

Elsewhere this messenger is called "the Angel of the Lord," which we have discussed in Section II. He is understood to be the pre-incarnate appearance of Christ, or a Christophany (Exod 33:14-15; Judges 6:12; Isa 63:9). The Messiah is the mediator of all the covenants of the Bible (Heb 8:8-13; 12:24); He is the communicator, executor, administrator, and consummator of that divine plan.

The Christophanies and especially the incarnation may be viewed as indispensable steps toward God's ultimate purpose of being with

His created people. Thus, God's desire as expressed in Revelation 21:3 will be realized.[70] There John says, *"And I heard a great voice out of heaven saying, Behold, the tabernacle of the God is with men, and He will dwell with them, and they shall be His people, and God Himself shall be with them, and be their God.*

The evidence of the Messiah in the Old Testament is simply overwhelming. In type, in form or in prophecy, the intricate detail, interrelationships, and historical evidence for the unfolding revelation of God's plan to send a Savior is evident from beginning to end. The gospel of Jesus Christ can be taught and understood without the aid of the New Testament, but God has given us both testaments. When you consider that the Bible was written over a period of 1,500 years by some 40 authors, most of which did not know one another, when you see the biblical consistency of the gospel story throughout, you wonder how any fair-minded man could miss the truth of it all.

We can see that the Old Testament foreshadows completely the coming of Christ. Perhaps the foretelling is completed in Jeremiah 31:31-34 where the prophet looks forward to the New Covenant. It is not so much that the New Covenant is complicated or difficult for us to understand; it is that it is so profound we scarce can take it in. The Old Covenant was of the Letter of the Law given to Moses and administered through the oft repeated priestly ritual for the covering of sins as a copy of the true sacrifice. The New Covenant is by the true mediation of the Blood of Jesus Christ, the sacrifice once and for all for the remission of sins, written on the minds and hearts of the believers through the eternal Spirit.

> *Christ has not entered the holy places made with hands, which are copies of the true, but into heaven itself, now to appear in the presence of God for us* (Heb 9:24).

One can only say that *"the people dwelling in darkness have seen a great light, and for those dwelling in the region and shadow of death, on them a light has dawned"* (Isa 42:7). Yet, *"the people loved the darkness rather than the light because their works were evil"* (John 3:19). But for the rest of us, *"since we are surrounded by so great a cloud of witnesses, let us also lay aside every weight, and sin which clings so closely, and let us run with endurance the race that is set before us, looking to Jesus, the author and Finisher of our faith, who for the joy that was set before Him endured the cross, despising the shame, and is seated at the right hand of the throne of God"* (Heb 1:1-2).

NOTES

Preface

1. Norman L. Geisler and William E. Nix, *A General Introduction to the Bible.* (Chicago: Moody Press, 1968, 1986), p.22
2. Willis J. Beecher, *The Prophets and the Promise*, Lightly Edited for the 21st C. (from the Stone Lectures, presented at Princeton Seminary in 1905). (Ancaster, ON: Alev Books, 2011), p.218.

Intro to Part I – CHRIST IN TYPE: THAT WE MAY UNDERSTAND

3. Edmund P. Clowney, *The Unfolding Mystery: Discovering Christ in the Old Testament*, 2nd Ed. (25th Anniversary Edition) (Phillipsburg, NJ: P&R Publishing, 1988, 2013), p.16.

Chapter 1 - The Covenant of Pieces

4. Ronald Hunter, *Delightful Insights: New Testament Truths in Old Testament Word Pictures* (Kearney, NE: Morris Publishing, 2014), p.23.
5. Clowney, op. cit., p.51.

Chapter 2 – The Slavery in Egypt

6. Hunter, op. cit., p.31

Chapter 3 – The Tabernacle

7. Walter C. Kaiser Jr., *The Promise-Plan of God* (Grand Rapids, MI: Zondervan, 2008), p.85.
8. Alex W. Ness, *Pattern for Living: The Tabernacle, Priesthood, Offerings and Feasts* (Ontario, Canada: Christian Centre Publications, 1979). Attribution is posted on this graphic. I could not find a source for permission from the publishers of this out of print book.
9. Biblq.net/answer/4024/ in answer to the question, *"Where did the Israelites get all the materials for the Tabernacle?"*
10. Hunter, op. cit., p.77.
11. I have adapted some of this information from *The Tabernacle Place* for the detail of the above discussion. Original URL: www.the-tabernacle-place.com/tabernaclearticles/what-is-the-tabernacle.aspx, 2004.

Chapter 4 – The Passover and Day of Atonement

12. www.jewsforjesus.org/judaica/passover (This brief explanation is found in a video presentation by Jews for Jesus.)
13. Craig Blaising, "Christ in the Old Testament," article in Holman Christian Standard Bible. (Nashville, TE: Holman Bible Publishers, 2010), p.1792.
14. Clint Patronella, *"The Gospel in the Day of Atonement,"* 2012. www.thevillagechurch.net/sermon/the-gospel-in-the-day-of-atonement/

Chapter 5 – The Feast of Tabernacles

15. Although the composer is unknown, this chorus is included in *Scriptures to Sing* (Kansas City, MO: Lillenas Publishing Co, 1977), p.90.
16. Hunter, op. cit., pp. 135-136.

Chapter 7 – The Lives of Christ-Like Men

17. Credit for Isaac as a type of Christ is given to Michal Hunt, http://www.agapebiblestudy.com/charts/Typology%20of%20Issac%20and%20Jesus.htm
18. I am indebted to www.learnthebible.org/like-unto-me-moses-as-a-type-of-christ.html for this list comparing Moses to Christ.
19. For these typologies in Boaz see www.nevadapilgrims.net/ruthses5.html.
20. For this discussion see www.discerningtheworld.com/images/wpi/SamuelatypeofJesusChrist.pdf.
21. For a fine sermon outline on *"David, a Man after God's Own Heart,"* see Executable Outlines, Mark A. Copeland, 2009. http://www.ccel.org/contrib/exec_outlines/text/1sa13_13.htm
22. For a discussion of the typology of Esther see http://www.scribd.com/doc/34412046/Typology-in-the-Book-of-Esther#scribd
23. *"Christ in the Scriptures,"* from the introduction to the book of Hosea in *New King James Study Bible*, 2d ed. Nashville: Thomas Nelson, 2007.

Intro to Part II

    24. James A. Borland, *Christ in the Old Testament: Old Testament Appearances of Christ in Human Form*, Revised and expanded edition (Chicago: Moody Press, 1999), pp.22-23.
    25. John F. Walvoord, "The Work of the Preincarnate Son of God," Bibliotheca Sacra 104, no.4 (October-December 1947):415.

PART II – CHRIST IN FORM: THAT WE MAY SEE

Chap 8 – Christophany (The Angel of Jehovah)

    26. Lewis Sperry Chafer, *Systematic Theology*, Vol. 2, (Grand Rapids, MI: Kregel Publications, 1993), p.8.
    27. John Walvoord, *Jesus Christ Our Lord*, new ed. (Chicago: Moody Publishers, 1969), p.54.
    28. Borland, op. cit., p.65.
    29. Borland, op.cit., pp.123-137. (for a historical view of the doctrine of Christophany)
    30. Wil Pounds, "*The Angel of the Lord*," a message at www.abideinchrist.com
    31. Robert Lightner, *Angels, Satan, and Demons*, (Nashville, TN: Word Publishing, 1998), pp.55-63.
    32. Ibid., p.165.
    33. Borland, op.cit., pp.43-44.
    34. Ibid. pp.38-43
    35. For the meaning of "first born" in this passage see Chapter 6, *The Theme of "Firstborn" in the Bible*.
    36. Borland, op.cit., p.107.
    37. Ibid. p.65.

Intro to Part III – CHRIST IN PROPHECY: THAT WE MAY BELIEVE

38. Walter C. Kaiser, Jr., *"Jesus in the Old Testament,"* Gordon-Conwell Theological Seminary resources. http://www.gordonconwell.edu/resources/Jesus-in-the-Old-Testament, 2009, p.1.
39. Clowney, op. cit., p.44
40. Kaiser, op.cit., *"Jesus in the Old Testament"*, p.2.

Chap 9 – Messianic Prophecy in the Pentateuch

41. Walter C. Kaiser Jr., *The Messiah in the Old Testament* (Grand Rapids, MI: Zondervan Publishing House, 1995) 38-39. I have used Dr. Kaiser's book as an organizational principle for Part III, which is outlined chronologically. Dr. Kaiser's book, which is more technical and learned than I can present here, also stands as a source for us all in seeing God's promise-plan as revealed through prophecy.
42. Ibid. p.39.
43. Ibid. pp.42-46.
44. Ibid. p.46
45. Ibid. pp.51-52.
46. Clowney, op. cit., p.87.
47. Kaiser, op.cit., *The Messiah in the Old Testament*, pp.53-57
48. Ibid. pp.57-60.
49. Walter C. Kaiser, Jr., *"Jesus in the Old Testament,"* Gordon-Conwell Theological Seminary resources. http://www.gordonconwell.edu/resources/Jesus-in-the-Old-Testament, 2009, p.2.
50. Kaiser, op. cit. *The Messiah in the Old Testament*, pp.61-64.

Chap 10 – Messianic Prophecy Leading up to David

>51. Kaiser, op.cit., *The Messiah in the Old Testament*, p.71.
>52. Ibid. p.78.
>53. Ibid. p.83.

Chap 11 – David & the Psalms

>54. J. Barton Payne, *Encyclopedia of Biblical Prophecy* (New York: Harper and Row, 1973), p.257.
>55. Kaiser, op. cit., *The Messiah in the Old Testament*, p. 101.
>56. Ibid., p.109.

Chap 12 – Ninth & Eighth Century Prophets

>57. Willis J. Beecher, op. cit., p.138.
>58. Ibid., p.138.
>59. Kaiser, op. cit., *The Messiah in the Old Testament*, p.140-141.
>60. See NET Bible, note on Joel 2:23 phrase "hammoreh litsdaqah." The translators of the NET Bible chose to render the phrase "early rains," although normally meaning "teacher of righteousness."
>61. Kaiser, op.cit., The Messiah in the Old Testament, p.142. (The "rain/teacher" poetic expression is found also in Isaiah 30:20,23).
>62. Ibid. p.143-144.

Chap 13 - Isaiah

>63. Kaiser, op.cit., *The Messiah in the Old Testament*, p.35. (Also see www.crivoice.org/branch.html)

64. "Who Has Believed," Words & Music by Marty & Jennifer Goetz, copywrite 1994 by Singin in the Reign Music/ASCAP.
65. Kaiser, op. cit., *The Messiah in the Old Testament*, p.178-181.

Chap 14 – Seventh & Sixth Century Prophets

66. Kaiser, op. cit., *The Messiah in the Old Testament*, p.193.

Chap 15 – Postexilic Prophets

67. Kaiser, op. cit., *The Messiah in the Old Testament*, p.207-208.
68. David Baron, *The Visions and Prophecies of Zechariah* (Grand Rapids: Kregel, 1972), p.149.
69. Kaiser, op. cit., *The Messiah in the Old Testament*, p.230.

Conclusion

70. Borland, op.cit., p.108

BIBLIOGRAPHY

Baron, David. *The Visions and Prophecies of Zechariah*. Grand Rapids, MI: Kregal, 1972.

Beecher, Willis J. *The Prophets and the Promise*, Lightly Edited for the 21st C. (from the Stone Lectures, presented at Princeton Seminary in 1905). Ancaster, ON: Alev Books, 2011.

Blaising, Craig. "Christ in the Old Testament," in Holman Christian Standard Bible. Nashville, TE: Holman Bible Publishers, 2010. (p. 1792)

Borland, James A. *Christ in the Old Testament: Old Testament Appearances of Christ in Human Form*, rev. Chicago: Moody Press, 1999, reprinted by Christian Focus Pub., 2007.

Bratcher, Dennis. *The Passover Seder for Christians*. CRI / Voice, Institute, last modified 2014.

Clowney, Edmund P. *The Unfolding Mystery: Discovering Christ in the Old Testament*, 2nd Ed. Phillipsburg, NJ: P&R Publishing, 1988, 2013.

Hunter, Ronald. *Delightful Insights: New Testament Truths in Old Testament Word Pictures*. Kearney NE: Morris Publishing, 2014.

Kaiser, Walter C. Jr. "Jesus in the Old Testament; Old Testament Appearances of Christ, Old Testament Predictions of the Coming Messiah," Gordon-Conwell Theological Seminary, 2009 (www.gordonconwell.edu/resources/Jesus-in-the-old-testament.cfm.)

Kaiser, Walter C. Jr. *The Messiah in the Old Testament*. Grand Rapids, MI: Zondervan Publishing House, 1995.

Kaiser, Walter C. Jr. *The Promise-Plan of God: A Biblical Theology of the Old and New Testaments*. Grand Rapids, MI: Zondervan Publishing House, 2008.

Kidd, George B. *Christophany: The Doctrine of the Manifestations of the Son of God under the Economy of the Old Testament.* London: Ward and Co., 1862; this reprint ed. by Kessinger Publishing, 2010.

Lightner, Robert. *Angels, Satan, and Demons.* Nashville, TN: Word Publishing, 1998.

Ness, Alex W. *Pattern for Living: The Tabernacle, Priesthood, Offerings and Feasts.* Ontario, Canada: Christian Centre Publications, 1979. "Old Testament Appearances of Christ." Christology, Lesson 4. (www.christology101.com)

Parsons, John J. *Worthy is the Lamb: A Messianic Passover Haggadah.* www.hebrew4christians.com, rev. 12, 2004.

Pounds, Wil. "*The Angel of God,*" message at www.abideinchrist.com

Walvoord, John F. *Jesus Christ Our Lord*, new ed. Chicago: Moody Publishers, 1969.

Walvoord, John F. "*The Work of the Preincarnate Son of God,*" Bibliotheca Sacra 104, no.4 (October-December, 1947):415.

ABOUT THE AUTHOR

Paul M. Ethington was born in 1946 in Illinois to a bi-vocational pastor/ teacher/ musician, Oakley Ethington. Raised in the Midwest, educated in California and Alaska, in and around the Church of the Nazarene, he developed a deep love for the Scriptures. For the last five decades he has conducted Bible Studies in small groups almost continuously. Squarely within orthodox Christianity he may be described as Wesleyan and an evangelical.

He obtained his B.S. in philosophy and M.S. in music from Cal State Fullerton. Although his vocation has been electrician, he is an avid reader whose hobby is biblical theology and passion is teaching. His habit of preparing his own curriculum and materials has led to many book manuscripts. Only recently has he attempted to publish. His penchant for taking complex material and organizing it for ease of understanding makes him very readable. He challenges his students to know Jesus more deeply as they go through life. He is not afraid to ask hard questions and to discuss Bible difficulties. His intention is to be more clear than clever and his style is expositional. He admits that he does not know everything, and that drives him to be an avid student who reads others' work. Yet, he is convinced that the Word of God is accessible to all and that remains his primary reference and focus; what do the Scriptures say? Mr. Ethington says that experience is instructive, though skewed. Tradition is important, though selective. Logic and conceptual analysis are helpful, though subject to artful manipulation. Only the Scriptures by the teaching of the Holy Spirit are trustworthy. With thorough exegesis Paul Ethington is determined to communicate this teaching to hungry hearts by the help of the Holy Spirit. He lives in Northern Idaho now with his wife Maria. Having spent most of their lives in SoCal and three years in Alaska, they are enjoying the four seasons. He has two grown children, Marisol and David. All of them are solid Christians active in their local settings. Still, there is a larger family who Mr. Ethington enjoys wherever he goes who love the Lord and look forward to His coming. His love for music allowed him to lead singing for forty years in the Church of the Nazarene. His love for people causes him to reach outside the walls of the church with frequent visits to missions where he plays the piano, sings and gives his testimony for the encouragement of all who seek Jesus.

Made in the USA
Monee, IL
29 April 2023

32592989R00105